FIRST PAST THE POST®

Numerical Reasoning:
Multi-Part

Multiple Choice
Book 2

How to use this book to make the most of 11 plus exam preparation

It is important to remember that for 11 plus exams there is no national syllabus, no pass mark and no retake option. It is therefore vital that your child is fully primed to perform to the best of their ability so that they give themselves the best possible chance on the day.

Unlike similar publications, the **First Past The Post®** series uniquely assesses your child's performance on a question-by-question basis, helping to identify areas for improvement and providing suggestions for further targeted tests. By entering the unique Peer-Compare™ access code for this book on our website, your child's performance can be compared anonymously to that of others who have taken the same tests.

Numerical Reasoning: Multi-Part

This collection of tests is representative of the multi-part numerical reasoning section of contemporary multi-discipline 11 plus and Common Entrance exams, which typically have two numerical reasoning papers. One paper usually contains long-worded numerical reasoning problems and the other usually contains short, quick-fire questions more akin to traditional maths. This book provides practice for the former question style. The answer to each question must be chosen from five possible options.

The suggested time for each test is based on data obtained from classroom-testing sessions held at our centre.

Never has it been more useful to learn from mistakes!

Students can improve by as much as 15%, not only by focused practice, but also by targeting any weak areas.

How to manage your child's practice

To get the most up-to-date information, visit our website, www.elevenplusexams.co.uk, the UK's largest online resource for 11 plus, with over 65,000 webpages and a forum administered by a select group of experienced moderators.

About the authors

The Eleven Plus Exams' **First Past The Post®** series has been created by a team of experienced tutors and authors from leading British universities.

Published by Technical One Ltd t/a Eleven Plus Exams

With special thanks to all the children who tested our material at the ElevenPlusExams centre in Harrow.

ISBN: 978-1-912364-37-4 (previously 978-1-908684-77-6)

Copyright © ElevenPlusExams.co.uk 2016

Second edition

elevenplusexams
head for success

About Us

At Eleven Plus Exams, we supply high-quality 11 plus tuition for your children. Our free website at **www.elevenplusexams.co.uk** is the largest website in the UK that specifically prepares children for the 11 plus exams. We also provide online services to schools and our **First Past The Post®** range of books has been well-received by schools, tuition centres and parents.

Eleven Plus Exams is recognised as a trusted and authoritative source. We have been quoted in numerous national newspapers, including *The Telegraph*, *The Observer*, the *Daily Mail* and *The Sunday Telegraph*, as well as on national television (BBC1 and Channel 4), and BBC radio. Our website offers a vast amount of information and advice on the 11 plus, including a moderated online forum, books, downloadable material and online services to enhance your child's chances of success. Set up in 2004, the website grew from an initial 20 webpages to more than 65,000 today, and has been visited by millions of parents. It is moderated by experts in the field, who provide support for parents both before and after the exams.

Don't forget to visit **www.elevenplusexams.co.uk** and see why we are the market's leading one-stop shop for all your 11 plus needs. You will find:

- ✓ Comprehensive quality content and advice written by 11 plus experts

- ✓ Eleven Plus Exams online shop supplying a wide range of practice books, e-papers, software and apps

- ✓ Lots of FREE practice papers to download

- ✓ Professional tuition service

- ✓ Short revision courses

- ✓ Year-long 11 plus courses

- ✓ Mock exams tailored to reflect those of the main examining bodies

Other Titles in the First Past The Post® Series
11+ Essentials Range of Books

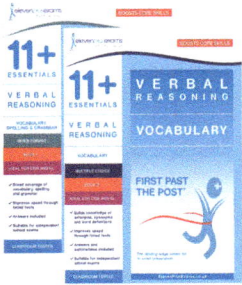

978-1-912364-60-2   Verbal Reasoning: Cloze Tests Book 1 - Mixed Format
978-1-912364-61-9   Verbal Reasoning: Cloze Tests Book 2 - Mixed Format
978-1-912364-78-7   Verbal Reasoning: Cloze Tests Book 3 - Mixed Format
978-1-912364-79-4   Verbal Reasoning: Cloze Tests Book 4 - Mixed Format
978-1-912364-62-6   Verbal Reasoning: Vocabulary Book 1 - Multiple Choice
978-1-912364-63-3   Verbal Reasoning: Vocabulary Book 2 - Multiple Choice
978-1-912364-64-0   Verbal Reasoning: Vocabulary Book 3 - Multiple Choice
978-1-912364-65-7   Verbal Reasoning: Vocabulary, Spelling and Grammar Book 1 - Multiple Choice
978-1-912364-66-4   Verbal Reasoning: Vocabulary, Spelling and Grammar Book 2 - Multiple Choice
978-1-912364-68-8   Verbal Reasoning: Vocabulary in Context Level 1
978-1-912364-69-5   Verbal Reasoning: Vocabulary in Context Level 2
978-1-912364-70-1   Verbal Reasoning: Vocabulary in Context Level 3
978-1-912364-71-8   Verbal Reasoning: Vocabulary in Context Level 4
978-1-912364-74-9   Verbal Reasoning: Vocabulary Puzzles Book 1
978-1-912364-75-6   Verbal Reasoning: Vocabulary Puzzles Book 2
978-1-912364-76-3   Verbal Reasoning: Practice Papers Book 1 - Multiple Choice

978-1-912364-02-2   English: Comprehensions Classic Literature Book 1 - Multiple Choice
978-1-912364-05-3   English: Comprehensions Contemporary Literature Book 1 - Multiple Choice
978-1-912364-08-4   English: Comprehensions Non-Fiction Book 1 - Multiple Choice
978-1-912364-14-5   English: Mini Comprehensions - Inference Book 1
978-1-912364-15-2   English: Mini Comprehensions - Inference Book 2
978-1-912364-16-9   English: Mini Comprehensions - Inference Book 3
978-1-912364-11-4   English: Mini Comprehensions - Fact-Finding Book 1
978-1-912364-12-1   English: Mini Comprehensions - Fact-Finding Book 2
978-1-912364-21-3   English: Spelling, Punctuation and Grammar Book 1
978-1-912364-00-8   English: Practice Papers Book 1 - Multiple Choice
978-1-912364-17-6   Creative Writing Examples

978-1-912364-30-5   Numerical Reasoning: Quick-Fire Book 1
978-1-912364-31-2   Numerical Reasoning: Quick-Fire Book 2
978-1-912364-32-9   Numerical Reasoning: Quick-Fire Book 1 - Multiple Choice
978-1-912364-33-6   Numerical Reasoning: Quick-Fire Book 2 - Multiple Choice
978-1-912364-34-3   Numerical Reasoning: Multi-Part Book 1
978-1-912364-35-0   Numerical Reasoning: Multi-Part Book 2
978-1-912364-36-7   Numerical Reasoning: Multi-Part Book 1 - Multiple Choice
978-1-912364-37-4   Numerical Reasoning: Multi-Part Book 2 - Multiple Choice

978-1-912364-43-5   Mathematics: Mental Arithmetic Book 1
978-1-912364-44-2   Mathematics: Mental Arithmetic Book 2
978-1-912364-45-9   Mathematics: Worded Problems Book 1
978-1-912364-46-6   Mathematics: Worded Problems Book 2
978-1-912364-52-7   Mathematics: Worded Problems Book 3
978-1-912364-47-3   Mathematics: Dictionary Plus
978-1-912364-50-3   Mathematics: Crossword Puzzles Book 1
978-1-912364-51-0   Mathematics: Crossword Puzzles Book 2
978-1-912364-48-0   Mathematics: Practice Papers Book 1 - Multiple Choice

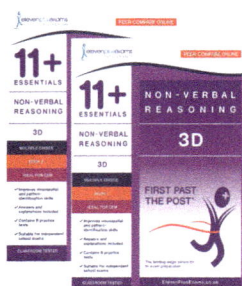

978-1-912364-87-9   Non-Verbal Reasoning: 2D Book 1 - Multiple Choice
978-1-912364-88-6   Non-Verbal Reasoning: 2D Book 2 - Multiple Choice
978-1-912364-85-5   Non-Verbal Reasoning: 3D Book 1 - Multiple Choice
978-1-912364-86-2   Non-Verbal Reasoning: 3D Book 2 - Multiple Choice
978-1-912364-83-1   Non-Verbal Reasoning: Practice Papers Book 1 - Multiple Choice

Contents

This workbook comprises 10 tests with 20 questions in each. Each test is designed to be completed in six minutes.

Glossary

Learn the meanings of the terms listed below to expand your mathematical vocabulary.

Apothem - a line segment from the centre of a regular polygon to the midpoint of one of its sides.

Bearing - an angle given in three figures that is measured clockwise from the north direction, e.g. 025°.

BIDMAS - an acronym for **B**rackets, **I**ndices, **D**ivision and **M**ultiplication, and **A**ddition and **S**ubtraction. It is the agreed order of operations used to clarify which should be performed first in a given expression.

Bimodal - when a collection of data has two modes, e.g. in the dataset: {1, 1, 1, 2, 4, 5, 5, 5}, the two modes are 1 and 5.

Bisect - to divide into two equal parts.

Coefficient - a constant that is placed before a variable in an algebraic expression, e.g. in the term $4x$, the coefficient is 4.

Complementary angles - two angles are complementary if they add up to 90°.

Cube number - a number that can be produced by multiplying another number by itself twice, e.g. 8 (= 2 × 2 × 2).

Edge - a line segment that joins two vertices of a 2D shape, or a line segment at which two faces meet in a 3D shape.

Enlargement - a type of transformation in which the size of an object is changed, whilst the ratio of the lengths of its sides stays the same.

Equidistant - two or more points are equidistant if they are the same distance from a common point.

Face - an individual surface of a 3D shape.

Fair - free from bias or equally likely to occur.

Gallon - a unit of volume used for measuring liquids. It is equal to 8 pints, or 4.55 litres.

Gradient - a measure of the steepness of a straight line.

Highest common factor (HCF) - the largest number that is a factor of two or more given numbers, e.g. 5 is the highest common factor of 10 and 15.

Imperial units - the system of units first defined in the British Weights and Measures Act. These units are no longer officially used in Britain, e.g. inches, feet, pints etc.

Inscribe - to draw a shape within another so that their edges touch, but do not intersect.

Integer - a whole number, i.e. not a decimal or a fraction.

Isosceles trapezium - a trapezium with one line of symmetry, two pairs of equal angles and one pair of parallel sides.

Leap year - a calendar year that occurs every four years. It has 366 days, instead of 365, and includes the 29th February. The year 2012 was a leap year.

Lowest common multiple (LCM) - the smallest number that is a multiple of two or more given numbers, e.g. 6 is the lowest common multiple of 2 and 3.

Metric units - a system of units based on multiples of 10, e.g. millimetre (mm), centimetre (cm) or metre (m).

Net - a 2D pattern that can be cut out and folded to make a 3D shape.

Parallel - lines that run side-by-side, always remain the same distance apart and never intersect, even if they are extended.

Perimeter - the total distance around the outside of a 2D shape.

Perpendicular - two lines are perpendicular if they are at an angle of 90° to each other.

Polygon - a 2D shape with three or more straight sides and no curved sides, e.g. triangle, pentagon, hexagon.

Polyhedron - a 3D shape whose faces are polygons, e.g. triangular pyramid, octahedron.

Prime factor - one of a collection of prime numbers whose product is a particular number, i.e. 2 × 2 × 3 = 12, so 2, 2 and 3 are the prime factors of 12.

Prime number - an integer greater than 1 that has no factors other than 1 and itself, e.g. 2, 3, 5.

Prism - a solid 3D shape with two identical, parallel end faces that are connected by flat sides.

Pyramid - a solid 3D shape whose base is a polygon and has triangular faces that meet at a single vertex.

Quadrilateral - a 2D shape with four straight sides. Quadrilaterals are polygons.

Reflective symmetry - a shape or an object has reflective symmetry if an imaginary line can be drawn that divides the shape into two, so that one half is a reflection of the other in the imaginary line.

Regular - a regular polygon has sides of equal length.

Remainder - a number that is left over after a division.

Rotational symmetry - a shape or an object has rotational symmetry if it can be rotated, but still appears to be in the same original position, e.g. a square has rotational symmetry of four, because it can be rotated four times, but still appears the same.

Scalene - the sides of a scalene triangle are all of different lengths.

Sequence - a list of numbers or objects arranged in a particular order, which is defined by a specific rule, or set of rules.

Square number - a number that can be produced by multiplying another number by itself, e.g. 16 (= 4 × 4).

Supplementary angles - two angles are supplementary if they add up to 180°.

Triangle - a 2D shape with three straight sides. Triangles are polygons.

Triangular number - a number that can be represented by a group of equally spaced points arranged in a triangle, e.g. 1, 3, 6: ● ∴ ∷

Vertex - a point at which two or more straight lines meet.

Place Value

The numerical value of a digit in a number.

For example, in the number 1234.567, the digit 3 has a place value of tens.

1	2	3	4	.	5	6	7
thousands	hundreds	tens	units	decimal point	tenths	hundredths	thousandths

Special Numbers

	1st	2nd	3rd	4th	5th	6th	7th	8th	9th	10th	11th	12th	13th	14th	15th	16th	17th	18th	19th	20th
even	2	4	6	8	10	12	14	16	18	20	22	24	26	28	30	32	34	36	38	40
odd	1	3	5	7	9	11	13	15	17	19	21	23	25	27	29	31	33	35	37	39
square	1	4	9	16	25	36	49	64	81	100	121	144	169	196	225	256	289	324	361	400
cube	1	8	27	64	125	216	343	512	729	1000	1331	1728	2197	2744	3375	4096	4913	5832	6859	8000
triangular	1	3	6	10	15	21	28	36	45	55	66	78	91	105	120	136	153	171	190	210
prime	2	3	5	7	11	13	17	19	23	29	31	37	41	43	47	53	59	61	67	71
fibonacci	1	1	2	3	5	8	13	21	34	55	89	144	233	377	610	987	1597	2584	4181	6765

Equivalent Decimals, Fractions & Percentages

percentage	5%	10%	15%	20%	25%	30%	35%	40%	45%	50%	55%	60%	65%	70%	75%	80%	85%	90%	95%	100%	150%
fraction	$\frac{1}{20}$	$\frac{1}{10}$	$\frac{3}{20}$	$\frac{1}{5}$	$\frac{1}{4}$	$\frac{3}{10}$	$\frac{7}{20}$	$\frac{2}{5}$	$\frac{9}{20}$	$\frac{1}{2}$	$\frac{11}{20}$	$\frac{3}{5}$	$\frac{13}{20}$	$\frac{7}{10}$	$\frac{3}{4}$	$\frac{4}{5}$	$\frac{17}{20}$	$\frac{9}{10}$	$\frac{19}{20}$	$\frac{1}{1}$	$\frac{3}{2}$
decimal	0.05	0.1	0.15	0.2	0.25	0.3	0.35	0.4	0.45	0.5	0.55	0.6	0.65	0.7	0.75	0.8	0.85	0.9	0.95	1	1.5

Mathematical Symbols

+	addition
−	subtraction
×	multiplication
÷	division
±	positive or negative
=	equals sign
<	less than
>	greater than
≈	approximately equal to
≤	less than or equal to
≥	greater than or equal to
≠	not equal to
a^2	squared number
a^3	cubed number
%	per cent
$\sqrt{a}$	square root
$\sqrt[3]{a}$	cubed root
$\dot{a}$	recurring number
$a:b$	ratio
$a°$	degrees
$\bar{a}$	mean
(x, y)	coordinates
⌐	right angle
$\binom{x}{y}$	column vector (column matrix)
$^a/_b$	fraction
$\{a, b\}$	dataset
π	pi

Equivalent Periods of Time

1 minute	60 seconds
1 hour	60 minutes
1 day	24 hours
1 week	7 days
1 year	12 months (365 days)
1 leap year	366 days
1 decade	10 years
1 century	100 years
1 millennium	1,000 years

Roman Numerals

When a symbol appears *after* a numerically larger symbol, their values are added. When a symbol appears *before* a numerically larger symbol, their values are subtracted.

1	I		40	XL
2	II		50	L
3	III		60	LX
4	IV		70	LXX
5	V		80	LXXX
6	VI		90	XC
7	VII		100	C
8	VIII		200	CC
9	IX		300	CCC
10	X		400	CD
20	XX		500	D
30	XXX		1,000	M

Time Conversion

24-hour clock	12-hour clock
00:00	12.00am
01:00	1.00am
02:00	2.00am
03:00	3.00am
04:00	4.00am
05:00	5.00am
06:00	6.00am
07:00	7.00am
08:00	8.00am
09:00	9.00am
10:00	10.00am
11:00	11.00am
12:00	12.00pm
13:00	1.00pm
14:00	2.00pm
15:00	3.00pm
16:00	4.00pm
17:00	5.00pm
18:00	6.00pm
19:00	7.00pm
20:00	8.00pm
21:00	9.00pm
22:00	10.00pm
23:00	11.00pm

Units of Measurement

	Metric system		Imperial system		
	Units	Conversion	Units	Conversion	Metric approximation
Mass	milligram (mg)	1mg = 0.1cg = 0.001g	ounce (oz)	$1oz = \frac{1}{16}$ lb	1oz ≈ 28g
	centigram (cg)	1cg = 10mg = 0.01g	pound (lb)	1lb = 16oz	1lb ≈ 0.45kg
	gram (g)	1g = 100cg = 0.001kg	stone (st)	1st = 14lb	1st ≈ 6kg
	kilogram (kg)	1kg = 1,000g = 0.001t	ton	1 ton = 160st	1 ton ≈ 0.91 tonne
	tonne (t)	1t = 1,000,000g = 1,000kg			
Length	millimetre (mm)	1mm = 0.1cm = 0.001m	inch (in or ")	$1in = \frac{1}{12}$ ft	1in ≈ 25mm
	centimetre (cm)	1cm = 10mm = 0.01m	foot (ft or ')	1ft = 12in	1ft ≈ 30cm
	metre (m)	1m = 100cm = 0.001km	yard (yd)	1yd = 3ft	1yd ≈ 91cm
	kilometre (km)	1km = 100,000cm = 1,000m	mile	1 mile = 1,760yd	1 mile ≈ 1.6km
Volume	millilitre (ml)	1ml = 0.1cl = 0.001l = 1cm^3	fluid ounce (fl. oz)	$1fl.\ oz = \frac{1}{20}$ pt	1fl. oz ≈ 28ml
	centilitre (cl)	1cl = 10ml = 0.01l = 10cm^3	pint (pt)	1pt = 20fl. oz	1pt ≈ 0.57l
	litre (l)	1l = 100cl = 0.001kl = 1,000cm^3	gallon (gal)	1gal = 8pt	1gal ≈ 4.5l
	kilolitre (kl)	1kl = 1,000l = 1,000,000cm^3			

Types of Angles

Zero angle

Equivalent to 0°

The angle AÔB is an example of a zero angle.

Acute angle

An angle greater than 0°, but smaller than 90°

Angle $c°$ (AÔB) is an example of an acute angle.

Right angle

An angle of 90°

Angle $d°$ (AÔB) is an example of a right angle.

Obtuse angle

An angle greater than 90°, but smaller than 180°

Angle $e°$ (AÔB) is an example of an obtuse angle.

Flat angle

An angle of 180°

The angle AÔB is an example of a flat angle.

Reflex angle

An angle greater than 180°, but smaller than 360°

Angle $f°$ (AÔB) is an example of a reflex angle.

Full rotation

A full turn, equal to 360°

Pairs of Angles

Alternate angles

Alternate angles are formed when a straight line crosses a set of parallel lines.

Alternate angles are always equal.

Corresponding angles

Corresponding angles are formed when a straight line crosses a set of parallel lines.

Corresponding angles are always

Complementary angles

Two angles that add up to 90°

Since $a° + b° = 90°$, they are complementary angles.

Supplementary angles

Two angles that add up to 180°

Since $a° + b° = 180°$, they are supplementary angles.

Opposite angles

Angles that are opposite each other when two lines intersect

Opposite angles are always equal.

Angles in a revolution

The angles formed when lines meet each other at a point, or intersect

All the angles in a revolution always add up to 360°.

2D Shapes

Figures with two dimensions: length and width.

Circle	Right-angled triangle	Equilateral triangle	Isosceles triangle	Scalene triangle
r = radius d = diameter The perimeter of a circle is its circumference.	One angle is a right angle (90°). The other two angles are complementary.	All three angles are equal (60°). All three sides are of equal length.	Two angles are equal. Two sides are of equal length.	No angles are equal. No sides are of equal length.
Square	**Trapezium**	**Rhombus**	**Parallelogram**	**Kite**
All four angles are equal (90°). All four sides are of equal length. The diagonals bisect each other at 90°.	One pair of opposite sides is parallel.	Opposite angles are equal. All sides are of equal length. The diagonals bisect each other at 90°.	Opposite angles are equal. Opposite sides are parallel and of equal length. The diagonals bisect each other.	Two of the opposite angles are equal. Two pairs of sides are of equal lengths. The diagonals intersect at 90°.
Regular pentagon	**Regular hexagon**	**Regular heptagon**	**Regular octagon**	**Regular nonagon**
All five angles are equal. All five sides are of equal length. The sum of the interior angles is 540°.	All six angles are equal. All six sides are of equal length. The sum of the interior angles is 720°.	All seven angles are equal. All seven sides are of equal length. The sum of the interior angles is 900°.	All eight angles are equal. All eight sides are of equal length. The sum of the interior angles is 1,080°.	All nine angles are equal. All nine sides are of equal length. The sum of the interior angles is 1,260°.

3D Shapes

Figures with three dimensions: length, width and depth.

Cylinder	Triangular prism	Cuboid/square prism	Pentagonal prism	Cone
two flat faces and one curved face no vertices two curved edges	five faces six vertices nine edges	six faces eight vertices twelve edges	seven faces ten vertices fifteen edges	one flat face and one curved face one vertex one curved edge
Triangular pyramid/ tetrahedron	**Square-based pyramid**	**Octahedron**	**Hemisphere**	**Sphere**
four faces four vertices six edges	five faces five vertices eight edges	eight faces six vertices twelve edges	one flat face and one curved face no vertices one curved edge	one curved face no vertices no edges

Area Formulae

Area of a regular polygon = $\frac{1}{2}$ × apothem × perimeter $= \frac{1}{2} \times a \times p$	Area of a triangle = $\frac{1}{2}$ × base × perpendicular height $= \frac{1}{2} \times b \times h$	Area of a circle = pi × radius^2 $= \pi \times r^2$
Area of a parallelogram = base × perpendicular height $= b \times h$	Area of a kite = $\frac{1}{2}$ × product of the two diagonals $= \frac{1}{2} \times a \times b$	Area of a quadrilateral = length × width $= l \times w$
Area of a rhombus = $\frac{1}{2}$ × product of the two diagonals $= \frac{1}{2} \times a \times b$	Area of a trapezium = $\frac{1}{2}$ × sum of the lengths of the parallel sides × perpendicular height $= \frac{1}{2} \times (a + b) \times h$	

Volume Formulae

Volume of a cuboid = length × width × height $= l \times w \times h$	Volume of a prism = area of cross-section × height $= B \times h$

Other Useful Formulae

Surface area of a 3D shape = sum of the areas of all the faces	**Perimeter of a 2D shape** = sum of the lengths of all the sides
$x°$ is an exterior angle. $y°$ is an interior angle. An exterior angle of a regular polygon = $\frac{360°}{\text{number of sides}}$ $= \frac{360°}{n}$ An interior angle of a regular polygon = $\frac{180° \times (\text{number of sides - 2})}{\text{number of sides}}$ $= \frac{180° \times (n - 2)}{n}$	Circumference of a circle = 2 × pi × radius $= 2 \times \pi \times r$

Probability

A measure of how likely it is that a particular event will occur.
The probability of event A happening, P(A), is given by: number of ways in which event A can happen ÷ total number of possible outcomes.

'And' rule	'Or' rule
The 'and' rule is used to find the probability of a combination of events occurring. The probability of events A **and** B happening is: P(A and B) = P(A) × P(B) The word 'and' is replaced by a multiplication sign.	The 'or' rule is used to find the probability of one or other event occurring. The probability of event A **or** B happening is: P(A or B) = P(A) + P(B) The word 'or' is replaced by an addition sign.
Tree diagram One way of illustrating the probabilities of different events occurring is by using branches on a tree diagram. Each branch represents one possible event and is labelled with its probability. e.g. a tree diagram illustrating two tosses of an unbiased coin	**Probability scale** A scale that ranges from zero to one and measures the likelihood of an event occurring.

Tree diagram

First coin toss   Second coin toss

head — 0.5 — head
0.5
head — 0.5 — tail

tail — 0.5 — head
0.5
tail — 0.5 — tail

You can use the 'and' rule and the 'or' rule with the tree diagram: multiply probabilities along the branches, and add probabilities down the columns.

Probability scale

impossible	improbable	equally likely	probable	certain
0	0.25	0.5	0.75	1

Picking out a black marble from a bag which contains only blue marbles

A fair coin landing on heads

Picking out a red marble from a bag which contains only red marbles

Remember that probabilities can be expressed as fractions, decimals or percentages.

Venn Diagrams

A diagram showing all logical relations for a collection of sets using overlapping ovals, non-overlapping ovals and a rectangular boundary.

e.g. a Venn diagram showing the first ten positive integers

The oval represents a set. A set is a collection of numbers that share a particular property. In this case, it is a set of triangular numbers.

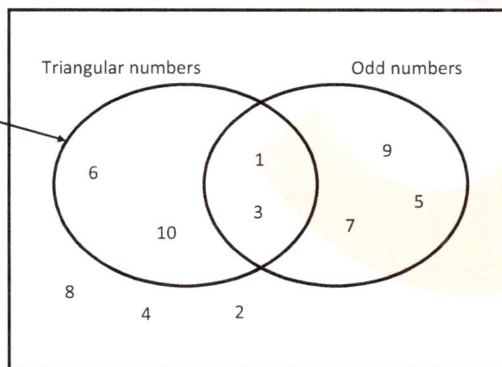

Triangular numbers: 6, 10, 8, 4
Odd numbers: 9, 5, 7
Intersection: 1, 3
Outside: 2

The rectangle represents the universal set.
The universal set contains all the elements in the sets within it.
In this case, it is the set of the first ten positive integers.

Some useful Venn diagram patterns:

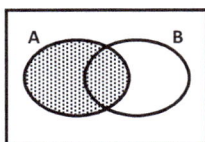

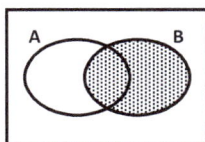

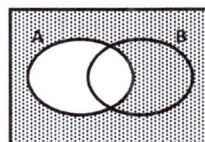

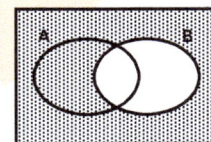

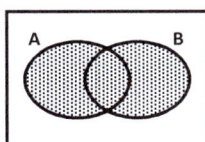

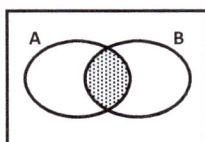

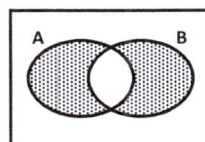

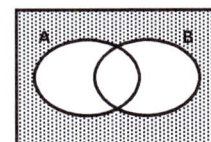

set **A**	set **B**	not **A**	not **B**

A or **B**	**A** and **B**	only **A** or only **B**	not **A** and not **B**

Instructions

Before starting each test, you will need the following:

1. a pencil

2. a rubber

3. a watch, clock or stopwatch

In this book, you are given options from which to choose your answers:

A	B	C	D	E
4.6%	6%	5%	3.2%	4.1%

To select your chosen answer, circle the letter above your chosen option:

A	B	C	D	E
4.6%	6%	5%	3.2%	4.1%

✓

Do not circle both the option letter and the answer, as this may cover the answer and make it unclear for marking.

A	B	C	D	E
4.6%	6%	5%	3.2%	4.1%

✗

If you want to change your answer, either rub it out or put a line through your original answer and circle the new answer.

A	B	C	D	E
4.6%	6%	5%	3.2%	4.1%

✗

A	B	C	D	E
4.6%	6%	5%	3.2%	4.1%

✓

A	B	C	D	E
4.6%	6%	5%	3.2%	4.1%

✓

Below are some **key points** to remember when attempting the tests:

i. Multi-part questions are longer questions with multiple parts to them, so making an error on one of the earlier parts can lead to more errors further on.

ii. Each test comprises **six multi-part questions** and should take **20 minutes** to complete. Ideally, each question should take around 30 seconds to solve. Therefore, it is essential that you work as quickly and carefully as you can.

iii. Calculators, rulers and protractors are **not permitted** in these tests. You should use the available space around the question to do your working.

iv. You should answer the questions in pencil. Thus, if you wish to change your original answer you will be able to rub it out.

v. If you are struggling with a question, move onto the next one to avoid wasting time. Time permitted, you can always return to any questions skipped.

Answers

To mark your work, use the 'Answers & Explanations' section at the back of this book. The mark scheme will tell you the correct answer option as well as a short explanation of why this is the case.

Question	Answer		Explanation
1	C	30	The highest common factor (HCF) is the largest whole number which is a factor of all the given numbers. Therefore, the HCF of 30, 60 and 150 is **30**.
2	A	6	The lowest common multiple (LCM) is the smallest whole number which is a multiple of all the given numbers. Therefore, the LCM of 2, 3 and 6 is **6**.
3	D	6	A prime number is a number that has only two factors; one and the number itself. Therefore only option D, **6**, is not a prime number.

BLANK PAGE

FIRST PAST THE POST®

Test 1

 **20 minutes**

Total

/30

Question 1

The following questions are based on the three calculations shown below.

Calculation X: £127 + £84 - £53

Calculation Y: (1.5 × 50cm) ÷ 10

Calculation Z: 12 × (96 ÷ 12 + 3) - 35

a.   What is the result of calculation X?

A	B	C	D	E
£144	£158	£171	£264	£185

b.   Calculation X is changed to £127 + (£84 - £53) - £1. What is the final result?

A	B	C	D	E
£170	£265	£143	£186	£157

c.   What is the result of calculation Y?

A	B	C	D	E
7.5cm	5.25cm	75cm	7.75cm	15cm

d.   If the divisor number 10 in calculation Y is halved, what is the new answer?

A	B	C	D	E
3.75cm	10.5cm	75cm	15.5cm	15cm

e.   Calculation Z requires number operations to be used in the correct order to obtain the right result. What is the right result?

A	B	C	D	E
64	-288	97	41.8	167

Question 2

The following questions refer to the shapes on the grid below.

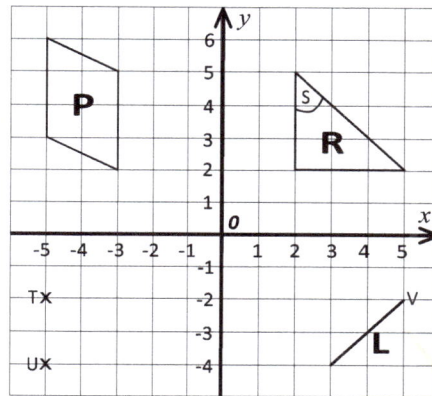

(Diagram not to scale)

a. What is the order of rotational symmetry of shape **P**?

A	B	C	D	E
1	2	3	4	5

b. If each small square on the grid has a width of 1cm, what is the area of shape **P**?

A	B	C	D	E
$8cm^2$	$6.5cm^2$	$7cm^2$	$6cm^2$	$7.5cm^2$

c. What is angle S in shape **R**?

A	B	C	D	E
35°	40°	60°	45°	50°

d. Points T and U are the two corners of the base line of an isosceles triangle. Which of these answers could be the coordinates of the third corner?

A	B	C	D	E
(-2, -3)	(-2, -1)	(4, -2)	(3, -4)	(2, -1)

e. If line **L** is rotated 90° anticlockwise about (3, -4), what are the coordinates of the end of the line V after rotation?

A	B	C	D	E
(3, -1)	(0, -4)	(4, -1)	(1, -3)	(1, -2)

Question 3

The following questions are based on the three sequences shown below.

Sequence P $\quad$ $\frac{1}{8}$ $\quad$ $\frac{1}{4}$ $\quad$ $\frac{3}{8}$ $\quad$ $\frac{1}{2}$ $\quad$ S $\quad$ $\frac{3}{4}$ $\quad$ $\frac{7}{8}$

Sequence Q

Sequence R $\quad$ T $\quad$ 3 $\quad$ 5 $\quad$ 7 $\quad$ 11 $\quad$ 13 $\quad$ 17 $\quad$ U

a. In sequence P, what is the value of the missing term S?

A	B	C	D	E
$\frac{4}{8}$	$\frac{9}{16}$	$\frac{5}{8}$	$\frac{5}{6}$	$\frac{2}{3}$

b. In sequence P, what is the sum of terms 3 and 6?

A	B	C	D	E
$1\frac{1}{4}$	1.5	$\frac{9}{8}$	$1\frac{1}{3}$	$\frac{6}{5}$

c. In sequence Q, how many smiley faces are needed to create term 4?

A	B	C	D	E
16	24	18	30	20

d. In sequence R, what is the lowest common multiple (LCM) of missing term T and term 2?

A	B	C	D	E
8	6	4	10	3

e. In sequence R, what are the factors of missing term U?

A	B	C	D	E
1 and 23	1, 2 and 11	1 and 29	1 and 19	1, 2 and 26

Question 4

Look at the two number machines labelled 1 and 2 below.

1 input $\Rightarrow$ ÷ 4 $\Rightarrow$? $\Rightarrow$ 27

2 1.5 $\Rightarrow$ × 6 $\Rightarrow$ - 12 $\Rightarrow$ + 18 $\Rightarrow$ output

a. If the input of number machine 1 is 12, which one of the following gives a possible instruction for operation 2?

A	B	C	D	E
+ 23	- 30	× 8	÷ 0.1	× 9

b. Using the information in part 4 (a) above, what is the input to output ratio for number machine 1?

A	B	C	D	E
4:9	5:8	12:18	5:9	15:27

c. In number machine 1, a new operation 2 instruction of + 7 is applied. What will the input need to be to keep the output at 27?

A	B	C	D	E
8.5	68	80	10.5	5

d. What is the output of number machine 2?

A	B	C	D	E
12	17	39	15	21

e. In terms of number value, what is the 5 worth in the input of number machine 2?

A	B	C	D	E
5 units	5 hundredths	5 thousandths	5 tenths	5 tens

Question 5

The bar chart below shows the number of cars sold by a garage over a six month period.

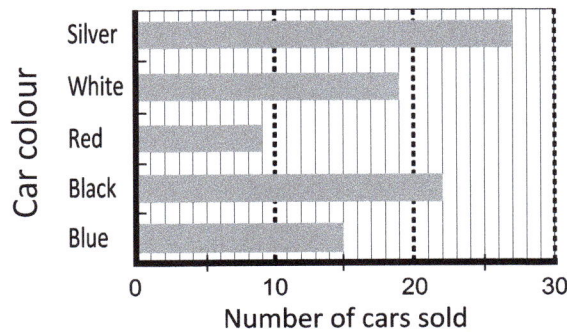

a. How many red cars and blue cars were sold in total?

A	B	C	D	E
31	24	15	28	22

b. How many more silver cars were sold than black cars?

A	B	C	D	E
8	5	12	3	6

c. How many cars were sold in total over the six month period?

A	B	C	D	E
83	101	92	96	89

d. During the following 6 months, the garage sold 50% more black cars. How many black cars were sold?

A	B	C	D	E
35	40	28	30	33

e. Two of the cars for sale weigh 1.08 tonnes and 1.5 tonnes respectively. What is the combined tonnage of both cars expressed in kilograms?

A	B	C	D	E
25,800kg	2,130kg	2,013kg	2,580kg	28,130kg

Question 6

The following questions relate to the 2D and 3D shapes shown below.

(Diagrams not to scale)

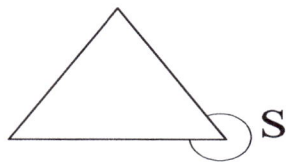

Shape 1

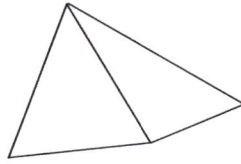

Shape 2

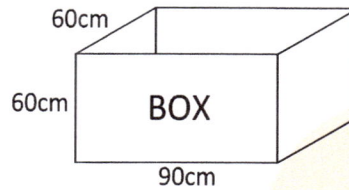

Shape 3

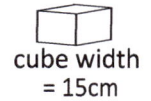

cube width = 15cm

a. Shape 1 is an equilateral triangle. What is angle S?

A	B	C	D	E
280°	315°	300°	260°	310°

b. What 2D shapes are required to form the net of the pyramid shown in Shape 2?

A	B	C	D	E
4 triangles, 1 square	2 squares, 3 triangles	4 triangles	1 rhombus, 4 trapeziums	1 oblong, 3 kites

c. For Shape 2, what is the number of faces + number of vertices - number of edges?

A	B	C	D	E
2	1	4	0	3

d. What is the area of the base of the large box shown as shape 3?

A	B	C	D	E
360cm^2	540cm^2	3,600cm^2	9,600cm^2	5,400cm^2

e. What is the maximum number of 15cm wide cubes that can be packed inside the large box shown as Shape 3?

A	B	C	D	E
108	96	64	144	84

BLANK PAGE

Test 2

 **20 minutes**

Total

/30

Question 1

The following questions refer to the number line and jug of water shown below.

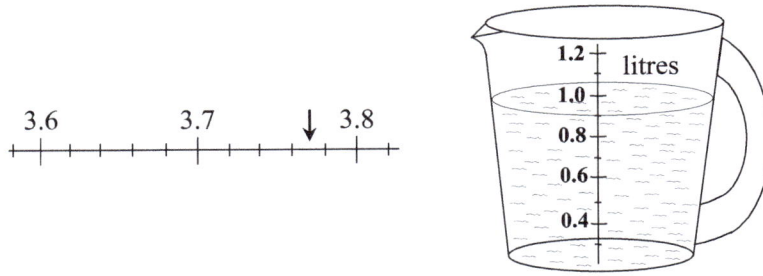

3.6   3.7   ↓ 3.8

1.2 — litres
1.0 —
0.8 —
0.6 —
0.4 —

a. Each large division on the number line above is split into five small divisions. What is one small division on the number line worth?

A	B	C	D	E
0.2	0.04	2	0.02	0.01

b. To what value is the arrow pointing on the number line?

A	B	C	D	E
3.73	3.735	3.77	3.75	3.707

c. Look at the value 3.6 on the number line. What is the 6 in this value worth?

A	B	C	D	E
$^6/_{1000}$	$^6/_{100}$	$^6/_{10}$	6	60

d. According to the scale, what is the quantity of water in the jug expressed in ml?

A	B	C	D	E
900ml	850ml	875ml	90ml	85ml

e. All the water in the jug is used to fill a number of 150ml capacity glasses. How many glasses are filled with water?

A	B	C	D	E
8	5	9	4	6

Question 2

The pie chart shows the number of electrical goods sold in one day.

Electrical Sales

(Diagram not to scale)

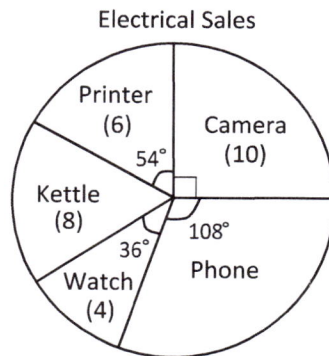

a. What angle should be assigned to the kettle sales on the pie chart?

A	B	C	D	E
60°	75°	68°	72°	78°

b. How many phones were sold during the one day period?

A	B	C	D	E
12	14	11	16	15

c. What percentage of all goods sold were watches?

A	B	C	D	E
12%	10%	15%	8%	11%

d. What is the mean of the five sales figures?

A	B	C	D	E
10	6	7	9	8

e. What is the product of the median and the range of the five sales figures?

A	B	C	D	E
9^2	6^2	7^2	5^2	8^2

Question 3

Jill is standing on the centre square of the number grid below. She selects one of the numbered grid squares at random.

49	4	7
27	🚶	64
1	14	15

N ↑

a.   What is the probability that she selects a square number?

A	B	C	D	E
$\frac{3}{8}$	$\frac{1}{2}$	$\frac{5}{8}$	$\frac{1}{4}$	$\frac{3}{4}$

b.   What is the probability that she selects a triangular number?

A	B	C	D	E
$\frac{1}{8}$	$\frac{5}{8}$	0	$\frac{1}{4}$	$\frac{3}{8}$

c.   Which of the following pairs of numbers taken from the number grid are consecutive?

A	B	C	D	E
1 and 7	7 and 27	15 and 27	14 and 15	14 and 49

d.   Jill wishes to walk from the centre square to a square with a prime number on it. In which direction should Jill walk?

A	B	C	D	E
NE	NW	E	SW	SE

e.   What fraction of the numbers on the grid are cube numbers?

A	B	C	D	E
$\frac{1}{4}$	$\frac{5}{8}$	$\frac{3}{8}$	$\frac{1}{2}$	$\frac{3}{4}$

Question 4

The following questions relate to the 2D shapes shown below.

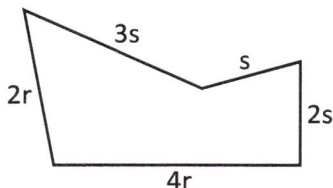

Shape 1a

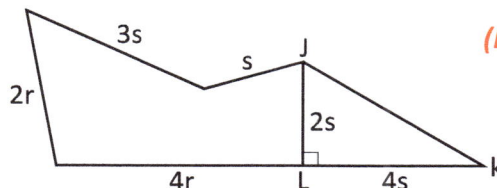

Shape 1b

(Diagrams not to scale)

a. What is the perimeter of shape 1a?

A	B	C	D	E
12rs	9(r - s)	2(3r + s)	5r + 6s	6(r + s)

b. The perimeter of shape 1a is 30cm and r = 3cm. What is the value of s?

A	B	C	D	E
1.8cm	3cm	2cm	2.2cm	1.5cm

c. What is the most suitable name for shape 1a?

A	B	C	D	E
Regular Pentagon	Irregular Heptagon	Irregular Pentagon	Trapezium	Irregular Nonagon

A triangle JKL is placed on the right-hand side of shape 1a to create shape 1b.

d. What is the length of the side of the triangle LK in centimetres (cm)?

A	B	C	D	E
8cm	6cm	10cm	7cm	9cm

e. What is the area of triangle JKL?

A	B	C	D	E
$32cm^2$	$8cm^2$	$12cm^2$	$16cm^2$	$20cm^2$

Question 5

The table below shows part of a train timetable.

	Train 1	Train 2	Train 3	Train 4
Oakdale	07:15	08:33	19:48	21:10
Cantlow	07:26	08:48	19:32	20:54
Bandford	07:35	08:55	19:24	20:47
Fulwood	—	09:02	19:19	20:41
Highlong	—	09:08	19:09	20:35
Langley	07:55	09:21	18:57	20:23

a. How many minutes does it take the 08:48 train from Cantlow to reach Highlong?

A	B	C	D	E
21	17	18	22	20

b. Ryan wishes to travel from Oakdale to Fulwood. At what time should he catch the train at Oakdale?

A	B	C	D	E
19:48	08:33	09:02	07:15	21:10

c. After a day of shopping, Nadia travels from Langley back home to Bandford, a train journey of exactly 24 minutes. At what time did Nadia catch the train at Langley?

A	B	C	D	E
20:23	18:57	20:47	09:21	19:09

A return train ticket from Oakdale to Langley costs £7.80 per adult and half the adult price for a child.

d. What is the total ticket cost for two adults and a child?

A	B	C	D	E
£23.40	£15.60	£19.50	£19.00	£21.50

e. How many seconds does it take train 4 to travel from Fulwood to Bandford?

A	B	C	D	E
300	290	370	360	340

Question 6

The following questions refer to the shapes on the grid shown below.

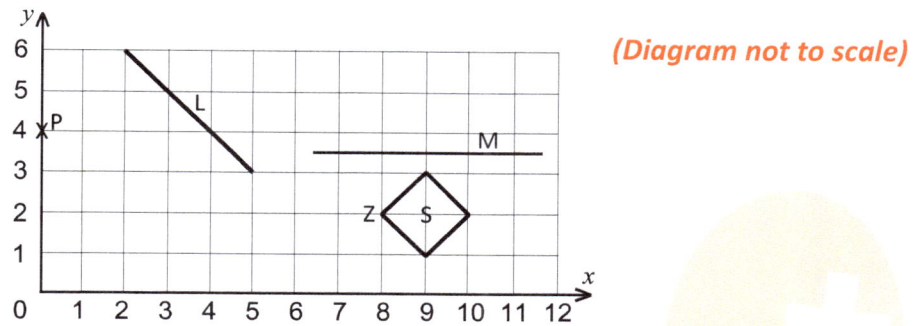

(Diagram not to scale)

a. What are the coordinates of point P?

A	B	C	D	E
(0, 4)	(4, 4)	(2, 0)	(4, 0)	(0, 2)

b. Point P is rotated 90° clockwise about the point (0, 0). What are the coordinates of point P after rotation?

A	B	C	D	E
(0, 4)	(4, 4)	(2, 8)	(4, 0)	(0, 8)

c. What are the coordinates at the centre of line L?

A	B	C	D	E
(4.5, 3.5)	(3, 5)	(4, 4)	(3.5, 4.5)	(5.5, 4.5)

d. Square S is reflected in the mirror line M. What are the coordinates of corner Z in the mirror image?

A	B	C	D	E
(10, 5)	(8, 5)	(9, 6)	(8, 4)	(9, 4)

e. For the square S, what is the sum of the number of lines of symmetry and the order of rotational symmetry?

A	B	C	D	E
6	8	4	10	12

BLANK PAGE

FIRST PAST THE POST®

Test 3

 **20 minutes**

Total

/30

Question 1

The rule used to find each term from the term before it in the sequence below is:

add 2 and then divide by 4

S   10   6   2   1   T

a.   Use the rule above to find the value of term T.

A	B	C	D	E
0	$\frac{3}{4}$	$-\frac{1}{4}$	$\frac{1}{4}$	$-\frac{3}{4}$

b.   What is the value of term S?

A	B	C	D	E
42	4½	38	22	½

c.   What is the lowest common multiple (LCM) of the second term and the third term in the sequence?

A	B	C	D	E
60	20	24	36	30

d.   What percentage of the six terms in the sequence are triangular numbers?

A	B	C	D	E
25%	33%	60%	45%	50%

e.   One of the terms in the sequence is a prime number? What term is it?

A	B	C	D	E
Term 1	Term 2	Term 3	Term 4	Term 5

Question 2

The following questions refer to the two shapes shown below.

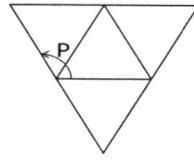 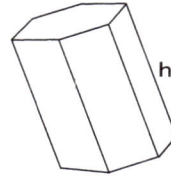

(Diagrams not to scale)

Shape 1   Shape 2

The net shown in Shape 1 has four identical equilateral triangles, each with a perimeter of 12cm.

a.   What is the distance around the outside edge of the whole net?

A	B	C	D	E
24cm	28cm	36cm	42cm	48cm

b.   What is angle P in Shape 1?

A	B	C	D	E
108°	130°	112°	120°	140°

c.   What is the name of the 3D shape formed when the net in Shape 1 is folded?

A	B	C	D	E
Irregular Tetrahedron	Square-based Pyramid	Triangular Prism	Regular Tetrahedron	Triangular-based Cone

The area of one end of Shape 2 is 11cm^2 and the height h is 7cm.

d.   What is the volume of Shape 2?

A	B	C	D	E
18cm^3	539cm^3	77cm^3	51cm^3	343cm^3

e.   How many edges does Shape 2 have?

A	B	C	D	E
12	18	15	6	24

Question 3

A group of children were surveyed, asking them their favourite food. The results are shown in the Venn diagram below.

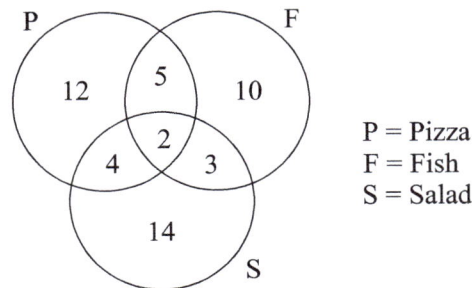

P = Pizza
F = Fish
S = Salad

a. How many children took part in the survey?

A	B	C	D	E
48	53	40	55	50

b. How many children eat Pizza?

A	B	C	D	E
21	12	23	14	26

c. Express the number of children that eat fish to the number of children that took part in the survey as a ratio in its simplest form.

A	B	C	D	E
2:5	3:5	2:3	1:5	6:25

d. How many children eat **only** salad?

A	B	C	D	E
14	16	18	10	12

e. How many children enjoy eating all three food types?

A	B	C	D	E
7	6	7	2	5

Question 4

The following questions refer to the diagrams shown below.

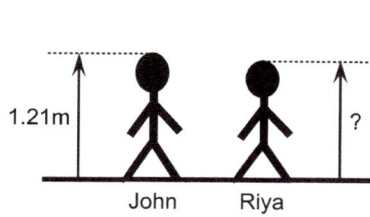

Figure 1

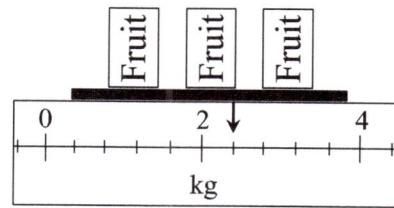

Figure 2

a. In Figure 1, Riya is 9cm shorter in height than John. How tall is Riya?

A	B	C	D	E
1.14m	1,120cm	1,140mm	1.12m	115cm

b. In Figure 1, what is John's height expressed in millimetres (mm)?

A	B	C	D	E
12,100mm	12.1mm	121mm	121,000mm	1,210mm

Figure 2 shows three identical tins of fruit on a weighing machine.

c. What is the mass of all three tins?

A	B	C	D	E
2.1kg	2.4kg	2.8kg	2.2kg	2.3kg

d. What is the mass of one tin expressed in grams (g)?

A	B	C	D	E
80g	600g	800g	6,000g	8,000g

e. What is the mass of 20 tins of fruit expressed in kg?

A	B	C	D	E
160kg	24kg	16kg	120kg	18kg

Question 5

Pari is revising algebra with the aid of the equations and expressions shown below.

$$1 \qquad 8x - 7 = 4x + 9$$

$$2 \qquad 3n + 2n = pt$$

$$3 \qquad (a + 9b)(2c - 3a)$$

For equation 1, Pari wants to move the $4x$ term to the left side of the equal sign.

a. Which of the options given below will achieve this aim?

A	B	C	D	E
Subtract $2x$ from	Multiply both	Add $4x$ to	Subtract $4x$ from	Divide both

b. Pari continues to rearrange equation 1 to find the value of x. What should x be?

A	B	C	D	E
4	5	16	8	2

c. What answer should Pari get when simplifying the left side of equation 2?

A	B	C	D	E
$5(1 + n)$	$6n$	$3 + 2n$	6	$5n$

d. Pari rearranges equation 2 to make n the subject of the formula. What answer should Pari get?

A	B	C	D	E
$n = 5pt$	$n = pt/5$	$n = 3pt/2$	$n = p2t/3$	$n = pt/6$

e. In expression 3, if $a = 1$, $b = 2$ and $c = 3$, what numerical result should Pari get?

A	B	C	D	E
22	60	57	31	54

Question 6

Anita spins the fair spinner below seven times and obtains the scores shown.

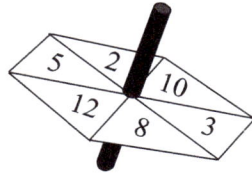

12   2   *N*   10   3   2   8

a.   What is the missing score *N* if the mean of all seven scores is 6?

A	B	C	D	E
3	10	5	8	12

b.   What is the mode score?

A	B	C	D	E
8	10	12	3	2

c.   What is the median score?

A	B	C	D	E
5	3	10	8	12

d.   What is the range of scores?

A	B	C	D	E
10	8	7	9	4

Anita spins the spinner one more time.

e.   What is the probability the score is an odd number?

A	B	C	D	E
$\frac{1}{2}$	$\frac{2}{3}$	$\frac{3}{7}$	$\frac{1}{3}$	$\frac{2}{7}$

BLANK PAGE

Test 4

 **20 minutes**

Total

/30

Question 1

Look at the three number machines labelled 1, 2 and 3 below.

| 1 | input $\Rightarrow$ instruction $\Rightarrow$ output |

| 2 | x $\Rightarrow$ × 6 $\Rightarrow$ - 2 $\Rightarrow$ 28 |

| 3 | 5 $\Rightarrow$ + 15 $\Rightarrow$ ÷ 0.5 $\Rightarrow$ × 0 $\Rightarrow$ output |

a. If the input to number machine 1 is 100 and the instruction is ÷ 0.25, what is the output?

A	B	C	D	E
4,000	250	125	400	25

b. If the output to number machine 1 is 100 and the instruction is ÷ 0.25, what is the input?

A	B	C	D	E
4,000	250	125	400	25

c. Which of the equations below is applicable to the setup of number machine 2?

A	B	C	D	E
$6x - 2 = 28$	$6x = 26$	$6 + x - 2 = 28$	$6x + 2 = 28$	$(6 ÷ x) + 2 = 26$

d. What is the input to number machine 2?

A	B	C	D	E
4.33	6	5	180	4

e. What is the output of number machine 3?

A	B	C	D	E
40	15.5	0	10	1

Question 2

The following questions relate to Figure 1 and Figure 2.

(Diagrams not to scale)

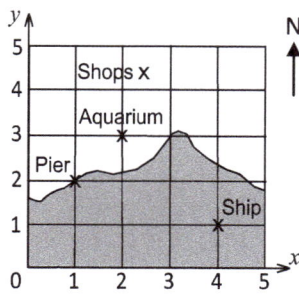

Figure 1

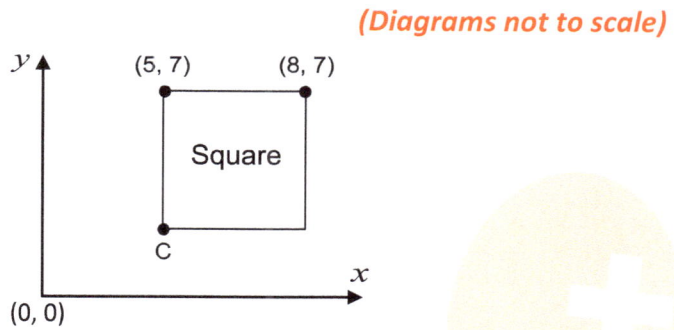

Figure 2

a.   What are the coordinates of the Aquarium in Figure 1?

A	B	C	D	E
(3, 2)	(2, 4)	(2, 3)	(1, 2)	(4, 1)

b.   In Figure 1, in which direction is the Aquarium from the ship?

A	B	C	D	E
SW	N	W	NW	NE

c.   In Figure 1, in which direction is the Pier from the Aquarium?

A	B	C	D	E
SW	S	SE	NE	W

d.   In Figure 2, what are the coordinates of corner C on the square?

A	B	C	D	E
(5, 3)	(4, 3)	(5, 4)	(7, 4)	(4, 5)

e.   In Figure 2, the square is translated three units to the left and one unit down. What are the new coordinates of corner C?

A	B	C	D	E
(4, 2)	(3, 2)	(3, 4)	(1, 3)	(2, 3)

Question 3

The tables below show data relating to the making and selling of pullovers.

Wool requirement per pullover

Age	6-8	9-11	12-14	15-16	Adult
Chest size (cm)	64	70	78	86	110
No. of 50g balls of wool	8	10	12	14	16
No. of 100g balls of wool	4	5	6	7	8

Pullover size	Cost per pullover
6-8 years	£4.50
9-11 years	£6.00
12-14 years	£7.50
15-16 years	£9.00
Adult size	£12.50

a. How many 50g balls of wool are required to make a pullover costing £9?

A	B	C	D	E
14	12	16	7	6

b. What is the cost of five pullovers for ages 12 - 14 years?

A	B	C	D	E
£30	£36.50	£38	£37.50	£62.50

c. Kim pays a total of £23 for one adult size pullover, one 9 - 11 size pullover and a third pullover. What was the size of the third pullover?

A	B	C	D	E
6 - 8	9 - 11	12 - 14	15 - 16	Adult

d. How many 100g balls of wool are required to make two adult size pullovers and one 12 - 14 size pullover?

A	B	C	D	E
16	28	14	23	22

e. 30kg of wool, in 100g balls, were used to make 12 - 14 size pullovers. How many pullovers were made?

A	B	C	D	E
40	50	48	60	56

Question 4

The following questions relate to the 2D and 3D shapes shown below.

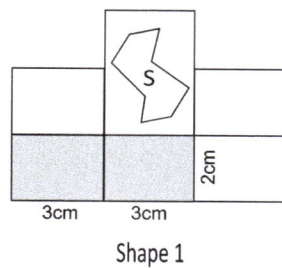

(Diagrams not to scale)

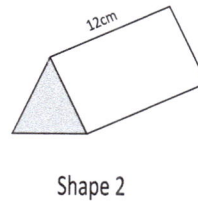

Shape 1   Shape 2

a.   What is the name of the 2D shape labelled S in Shape 1?

A	B	C	D	E
Irregular Heptagon	Regular Nonagon	Regular Trapezium	Irregular Rhombus	Irregular Octagon

b.   What is the perimeter of one of the shaded rectangles in Shape 1?

A	B	C	D	E
12cm	10cm	24cm	6cm	20cm

c.   What is the area of the two shaded rectangles in Shape 1?

A	B	C	D	E
$12cm^2$	$24cm^2$	$36cm^2$	$6cm^2$	$9cm^2$

d.   What is the name of the 3D shape shown in Shape 2?

A	B	C	D	E
Pentagonal Prism	Square-based Pyramid	Triangular Prism	Regular Cone	Triangular-based Pyramid

e.   The area of the shaded end of Shape 2 is $10cm^2$. What is the volume of shape 2?

A	B	C	D	E
$108cm^3$	$22cm^3$	$120cm^3$	$10.8cm^3$	$1,200cm^3$

Question 5

The diagrams represent a fair die and four cards from a standard pack of 52 playing cards.

The die shown above is rolled.

a.   What is the probability the score is greater than 2?

A	B	C	D	E
$^1/_2$	$^1/_3$	$^1/_6$	$^5/_6$	$^2/_3$

b.   What is the probability the score is a prime number?

A	B	C	D	E
$^1/_2$	$^1/_3$	$^1/_6$	$^2/_3$	$^5/_6$

c.   If the die is rolled twice, what is the probability of obtaining a 3 on both occasions?

A	B	C	D	E
$^1/_6$	$^5/_{12}$	$^5/_{36}$	$^1/_3$	$^1/_{36}$

The four playing cards shown above are removed from the 52 card pack.

d.   What is the probability of randomly selecting an Ace from the remaining cards in the pack?

A	B	C	D	E
$^1/_{12}$	$^1/_{26}$	$^1/_{25}$	$^1/_{16}$	$^2/_{49}$

One card is selected at random from the four playing cards shown above.

e.   What is the probability it is a black card?

A	B	C	D	E
$^1/_4$	1	$^1/_2$	0	$^3/_4$

Question 6

There are 96 counters in a bag, some coloured blue, some coloured red. The ratio of blue to red counters is 7:9.

a. How many blue counters are in the bag?

A	B	C	D	E
38	42	41	58	54

b. What is the difference between the number of red counters and the number of blue counters?

A	B	C	D	E
16	13	12	14	11

c. What fraction of all the counters are red?

A	B	C	D	E
$^7/_{12}$	$^7/_{16}$	$^{11}/_{16}$	$^7/_9$	$^9/_{16}$

d. What percentage of all the counters are blue?

A	B	C	D	E
43.75%	12.5%	60.25%	56.25%	34.75%

e. In terms of number value, what is the 6 worth in the number 96?

A	B	C	D	E
6 units	6 tenths	6 tens	6 hundred	6 hundredths

BLANK PAGE

FIRST PAST THE POST®

Test 5

 **20 minutes**

Total

/30

Question 1

The shape below is made up of one square of perimeter 168cm and four identical equilateral triangles.

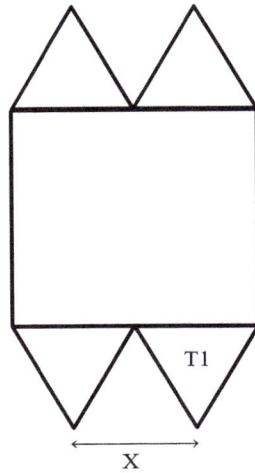

(Diagram not to scale)

T1

X

a. What is the length of one side of the square?

Ⓐ	B	C	D	E
42cm	48cm	84cm	51cm	40cm

b. How many lines of symmetry does the shape have?

A	B	Ⓒ	D	E
4	1	2	3	5

c. What is length X?

A	B	Ⓒ	D	E
18.9cm	15.5cm	21cm	10.5cm	20cm

d. What is the area of the square?

A	Ⓑ	C	D	E
2,304cm^2	1,764cm^2	1,698cm^2	1,761cm^2	1,752cm^2

e. What is the area of the square to the nearest 100cm^2?

A	B	C	D	Ⓔ
1,900cm^2	1,700cm^2	2,300cm^2	1,600cm^2	1,800cm^2

Question 2

Six fractions are shown below.

$$\frac{1}{2} \quad \frac{3}{8} \quad \frac{5}{6} \quad \frac{3}{4} \quad \frac{2}{5} \quad \frac{1}{3}$$

a. Which one of the six fractions is equivalent to $\frac{36}{96}$?

$\frac{36 \div 12 = 3}{96 \div 12 = 8}$

A	B	C	D	(E)
$\frac{3}{4}$	$\frac{1}{2}$	$\frac{5}{6}$	$\frac{2}{5}$	$\frac{3}{8}$

b. Which one of the six fractions is closest to 1 in terms of its value?

A	B	C	(D)	E
$\frac{3}{8}$	$\frac{3}{4}$	$\frac{1}{3}$	$\frac{5}{6}$	$\frac{2}{5}$

c. What is the result of adding together the two largest valued fractions from the set of six?

(A)	B	C	D	E
$\frac{19}{12}$	$\frac{4}{3}$	$\frac{37}{30}$	$\frac{2}{6}$	$\frac{17}{24}$

d. What is the result of multiplying the smallest valued fraction from the set of six by 108?

A	B	C	(D)	E
28	40.5	54	36	43.2

e. Which one of the six fractions when added to $1\frac{1}{4}$ gives $1\frac{3}{4}$?

A	(B)	C	D	E
$\frac{1}{3}$	$\frac{1}{2}$	$\frac{3}{4}$	$\frac{5}{6}$	$\frac{2}{5}$

Question 3

Two number machines labelled 1 and 2 are shown below.

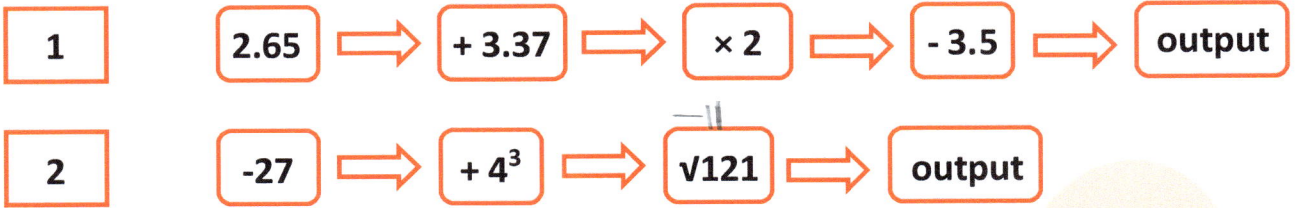

| 1 | 2.65 ⇒ | + 3.37 ⇒ | × 2 ⇒ | - 3.5 ⇒ | output |

| 2 | -27 ⇒ | + 4³ ⇒ | √121 ⇒ | output |

a. What is the output to number machine 1?

A	B	C	D	E
8.54	8.24	9.14	8.02	8.62

b. What is the input to number machine 1 rounded to the nearest whole number?

A	B	C	D	E
2	9	3.5	3	8

c. What is the output to number machine 2?

A	B	C	D	E
25	24.9	26	23	-26

d. What is the highest common factor of 39 and the output to number machine 2?

A	B	C	D	E
39	1,014	3	26	13

e. What is 90% of the input to number machine 2?

A	B	C	D	E
-24.3	-25	-24.7	-20.8	-23.4

Question 4

Felix writes down the first four terms of a number sequence.

5cm   100cm   20cm

500mm   **1m**   **150cm**   **2,000mm**

a. What is added to each term to obtain the next term?

A	B	C	D	E
50cm	60cm	150cm	200cm	75cm

b. What is the mean measurement of the first four terms of the number sequence?

A	B	C	D	E
115cm	112.5cm	100cm	118cm	125cm

c. What is the ratio of the first term in the number sequence to the third term in the number sequence?

A	B	C	D	E
1:2	500:150	3:1	1:3	1:150

d. What is the next term in the number sequence in kilometres?

A	B	C	D	E
2km	0.0025km	0.025km	0.2km	0.02km

e. Felix adds the second term in the number sequence to Y metres and gets 275 centimetres. What is the value of Y?

A	B	C	D	E
1.25m	1.95m	1.75m	1m	1.35m

Question 5

Tammy puts the following 3D toy shapes into a bag.

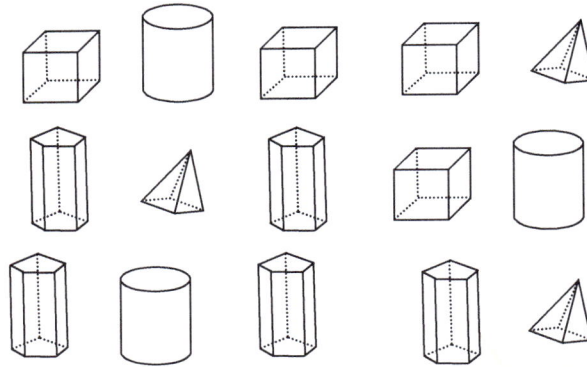

a. The four cubes shown in the diagram above are identical in size. They have a combined volume of 32,000mm^3. What is the length of an edge on one of the cubes?

A	B	C	D	E
2.5cm	1cm	2cm	1.5cm	0.5cm

b. How many edges are there in total on the three square based pyramids?

A	B	C	D	E
32	40	15	24	8

c. If Tammy were to select a shape at random from the bag, then what is the probability that she would select a pentagonal prism?

A	B	C	D	E
$\frac{1}{2}$	$\frac{1}{4}$	$\frac{1}{3}$	$\frac{5}{16}$	$\frac{1}{5}$

d. If Tammy were to select a shape at random from the bag, then what is the probability that it would have 4 or more faces?

A	B	C	D	E
$\frac{1}{2}$	$\frac{8}{15}$	1	$\frac{2}{3}$	$\frac{4}{5}$

e. How many vertices are there in total on the five pentagonal prisms?

A	B	C	D	E
50	40	25	75	35

Question 6

The grid below shows six points labelled P, Q, R, S, T and U.

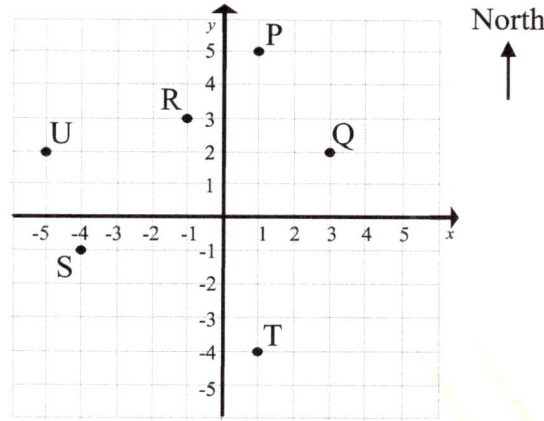

a. What are the coordinates of point U?

A	B	C	D	E
(-5, 2)	(-4, 1)	(2, -5)	(-5, -2)	(-4, -1)

b. If point R is reflected in the *y*-axis, then what are its new coordinates?

A	B	C	D	E
(3, 1)	(-1, 5)	(-1, -3)	(1, 3)	(-3, 1)

c. What point is 5 units right and 3 units down from point S?

A	B	C	D	E
R	T	S	Q	P

d. Point Q is rotated 180° clockwise about (0, 0), what are its new coordinates?

A	B	C	D	E
(2, -3)	(-2, -3)	(-3, -2)	(3, 2)	(2, 3)

e. What lettered point is directly North of coordinates (1, 4)?

A	B	C	D	E
R	U	T	P	S

BLANK PAGE

Test 6

 **20 minutes**

Total

/30

Question 1

The diagram below shows a trapezium, drawn in the scale of 1:6000 of a real life swimming pool of this shape. The trapezium is made up of a rectangle R and two identical triangles, T1 and T2.

(Diagram not to scale)

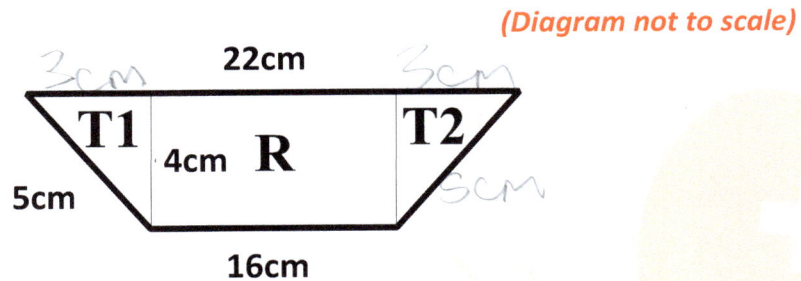

a. What is the area of triangle T1 in the drawing?

(A)	B	C	D	E
6cm^2	12cm^2	20cm^2	16cm^2	9cm^2

b. What is the area of rectangle R in the drawing?

A	(B)	C	D	E
48cm^2	64cm^2	20cm^2	88cm^2	12cm^2

c. What is the area of the trapezium in the drawing?

A	B	C	(D)	E
74cm^2	70cm^2	88cm^2	76cm^2	100cm^2

d. What is the perimeter of the trapezium in the drawing?

A	(B)	C	D	E
52cm	48cm	44cm	46cm	42cm

e. What is the actual scaled perimeter of the trapezium swimming pool in metres?

A	B	C	D	(E)
2,860m	2,755m	2,650m	2,910m	2,880m

Question 2

The bar chart below shows the number of spelling errors per page in an eight page leaflet.

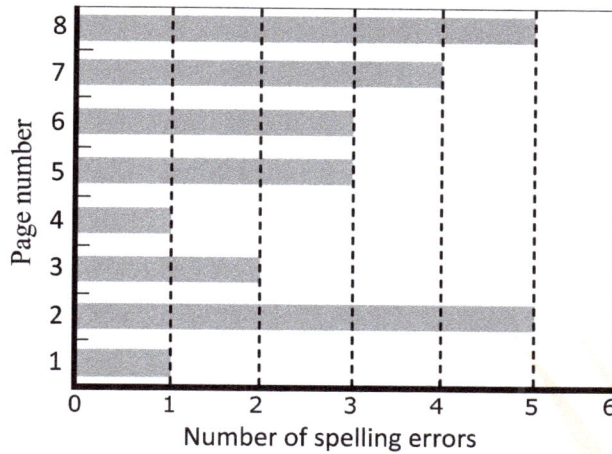

Page number (y-axis), values 1–8
Number of spelling errors (x-axis), values 0–6

54331251

a. How many of the pages in the leaflet had more than 2 spelling errors on them?

A	B	C	D	E
0	5	3	4	6

b. What was the median number of spelling errors per page in the leaflet?

A	B	C	D	E
5	4	3	0	2

c. What percentage of pages in the leaflet had one spelling error on them?

A	B	C	D	E
32%	35%	30%	25%	12.5%

d. What was the mean number of spelling errors per page in the leaflet?

A	B	C	D	E
5	2	1	3	4

e. What fraction of pages in the leaflet had between 2 and 4 spelling errors on them?

A	B	C	D	E
$\frac{1}{2}$	$\frac{3}{4}$	$\frac{1}{4}$	$\frac{1}{3}$	$\frac{3}{8}$

Question 3

Melody has 12 blank DVDs and 8 blank CDs in her possession. She purchased the DVDs for £4.50 each and the CDs for £3.25 each.

a. How much did she spend in total purchasing the DVDs and CDs?

A	B	C	D	E
£78	£68	£65	£80	£75

b. What is the ratio of DVDs to CDs that Melody has in her possession?

A	B	C	D	E
8:120	4:3	12:20	3:5	3:2

c. Melody records a film onto one of the DVDs. The film is exactly 90 minutes in length and the DVD has room on it for up to three hours of recorded material. What percentage of the DVD's playing time is taken up by the film?

A	B	C	D	E
50%	48%	25%	30%	55%

d. Each CD has a circumference of 37.6847cm. What is the circumference of a CD correct to three decimal places?

A	B	C	D	E
38cm	37.685cm	37.7cm	37.68cm	37.684cm

e. The diameter of a DVD is 11.87cm. What is the result of decreasing the DVD diameter length by 99 millimetres?

A	B	C	D	E
1.97cm	10.88cm	1.2cm	21.77cm	87.13mm

Question 4

The train timetable below shows some of the stations between Hammersmith and Barking. A train leaves Hammersmith at 14:44 and heads towards its next station, Gloucester Road.

Station	Arrival time
Gloucester Road	14:50
Victoria	14:58
Westminster	15:02
Tower Hill	15:14
Mile End	15:22
West Ham	15:26
Barking	15:28

a. How long does the train take to travel between Hammersmith and Barking?

A	B	C	D	E
41 min	58 min	38 min	54 min	44 min

b. A quarter of an hour after leaving Hammersmith, an inspector starts inspecting passenger tickets on the train. What time does the ticket inspection begin?

A	B	C	D	E
15:14	15:04	14:59	15:05	14:55

c. What time will the train arrive at Tower Hill station in 12 hour clock format?

A	B	C	D	E
5:14 PM	2:14 PM	3:45 PM	1:14 PM	3:14 PM

d. When the train arrives at Barking it will be serviced for 900 seconds. How long will the servicing take in minutes?

A	B	C	D	E
10 min	15 min	19 min	12 min	9 min

e. One of the posters on the train shows the fractional problem $\frac{1}{2} - \frac{1}{5}$. What is the answer to this problem?

A	B	C	D	E
$\frac{3}{10}$	$\frac{2}{15}$	$-\frac{1}{3}$	0	$\frac{2}{5}$

Question 5

The first five terms of a number sequence are shown below.

$$\times 3 \quad \times 3 \quad \times 3 \quad \times 3$$

0.5   1.5   4.5   13.5   40.5

a.   What is the range of the first five terms of the number sequence?

A	B	C	D	E
40	39	40.5	4	41

b.   What is the sixth term in the number sequence?

A	B	C	D	E
121.5	40.5	54	120	115.5

c.   Amit thinks of a number and multiplies it by 3. He then adds 4.5 to the result to get the fourth term in the number sequence above. What number did he think of?

A	B	C	D	E
5	0.5	1.5	3	7

d.   What is the result of multiplying the 1800th term in the sequence by zero?

A	B	C	D	E
180	8	0	18	1

e.   How much above -0.25 is the first term in the number sequence?

A	B	C	D	E
0.3	1	0.75	0.25	0.65

Question 6

A cuboid, cylinder and cone are shown below.

(Diagrams not to scale)

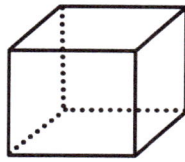

a. The volume of the cuboid is 300cm³. Its height is 10cm and its width is 2cm. What is its length?

A	B	C	D	E
8cm	20cm	25cm	30cm	15cm

b. If 1 inch ≈ 2.5cm and 1 foot = 12 inches then what is the approximate height of the cuboid in feet?

A	B	C	D	E
0.35 feet	0.17 feet	0.33 feet	0.4 feet	0.47 feet

c. The volume of the cylinder is three times the volume of the cone. If the volume of the cylinder is 138cm³, then what is the volume of the cone?

A	B	C	D	E
46cm³	48cm³	23cm³	414cm³	40cm³

d. The weight of the cone is 555,000 milligrams. What is its weight in kilograms?

A	B	C	D	E
0.555kg	5.55kg	555kg	0.0555kg	55.5kg

e. On the cuboid each face has either a 1 or 2 written on it. The number 1 is only written on 2 faces. How many faces have the number 2 written on them?

A	B	C	D	E
0	3	1	2	4

BLANK PAGE

FIRST PAST THE POST®

Test 7

 **20 minutes**

Total

/30

Question 1

A jug of water is shown below.

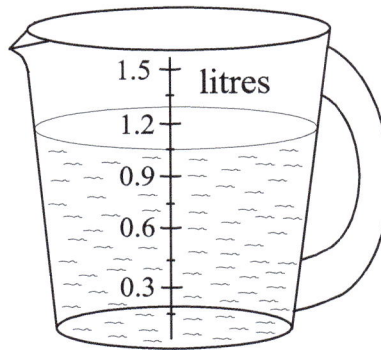

a. How much water is in the jug in millilitres?

A	B	C	D	E
1,500ml	1,050ml	1,000ml	1,005ml	975ml

b. What percentage of the 1.5 litre jug is filled to capacity with water?

A	B	C	D	E
68%	55%	70%	65%	90%

c. If the jug shown above was emptied and refilled with water to $^3/_5$ of its 1.5 litre capacity, then how much liquid would it contain?

A	B	C	D	E
0.95 litres	1.0 litres	0.99 litres	1.2 litres	0.9 litres

d. If the jug shown above was emptied and refilled with water to contain 600ml, then how much liquid would need to be removed to reduce the amount of water in the jug to 0.15 litres?

A	B	C	D	E
450ml	150ml	425ml	300ml	125ml

e. If 1 pint ≈ 500ml, then a full jug of 1.5 litres of water contains approximately how many pints of water?

A	B	C	D	E
1 pint	5 pints	3 pints	1.5 pints	2 pints

Question 2

The values on the counters below form a number set.

$$27 \quad 31 \quad 15 \quad 10 \quad 4 \quad 25 \quad 21$$

The counters are all placed in a bag and one counter is drawn out at random.

a. What is the probability that a triangular number is drawn out?

A	B	C	D	E
$^1/_7$	$^4/_7$	0	$^2/_7$	$^3/_7$

b. What is the probability that a squared number is drawn out?

A	B	C	D	E
$^4/_7$	$^3/_7$	$^2/_7$	$^1/_7$	0

c. What is the probability that a cubed number is drawn out?

A	B	C	D	E
$^4/_7$	$^2/_7$	$^3/_7$	0	$^1/_7$

d. The counter drawn out has 31 on it. What is 31 in Roman numerals?

A	B	C	D	E
XXXI	XXIX	VI	XXVIII	XXIII

e. What is the average of the seven values on the counters?

A	B	C	D	E
20	19	10	27	21

Question 3

A regular hexagon with corner points P, Q, R, S, T and U is shown below.

(Diagram not to scale)

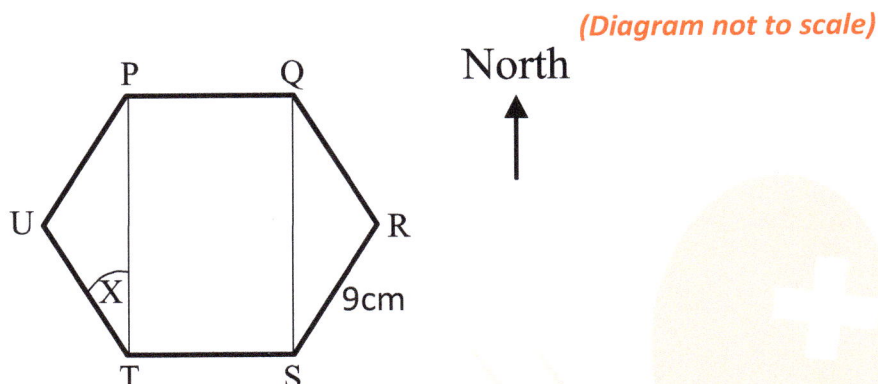

a. How many lines of symmetry does a regular hexagon have?

A	B	C	D	E
6	12	9	3	8

b. Which line is parallel to line TU?

A	B	C	D	E
PU	RS	QR	ST	PQ

c. Which corner point is directly south of point P?

A	B	C	D	E
S	U	Q	T	R

d. What is the size of angle X?

A	B	C	D	E
30°	12.5°	15°	45°	28°

e. What is the perimeter of the hexagon in millimetres?

A	B	C	D	E
790mm	540mm	900mm	580mm	450mm

Question 4

Three number machines are shown below, labelled 1, 2 and 3.

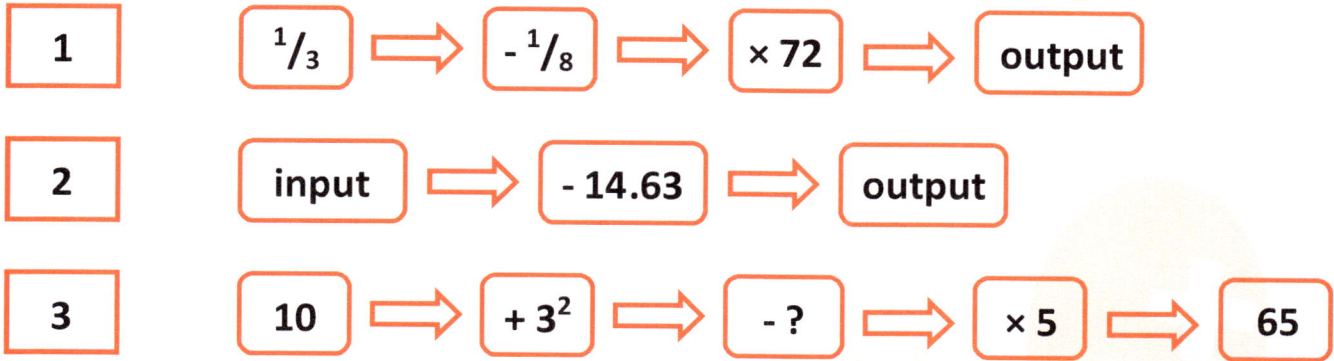

| 1 | | $^1/_3$ ⇒ $-^1/_8$ ⇒ × 72 ⇒ output |

| 2 | | input ⇒ - 14.63 ⇒ output |

| 3 | | 10 ⇒ + 3² ⇒ - ? ⇒ × 5 ⇒ 65 |

a. What is the following ratio?

Output to number machine 3:input to number machine 3

A	B	C	D	E
5:65	10:75	18:17	13:2	10:55

b. What is the output to number machine 1?

A	B	C	D	E
10	15	13	14.4	8.8

c. What is the input to number machine 2?

A	B	C	D	E
26.5	18.22	-2.76	28.43	22.5

d. What number is represented by the question mark in number machine 3?

A	B	C	D	E
8	6	12	10	4

e. What is the output to number machine 2 rounded to the nearest tenth?

A	B	C	D	E
10	11.7	12	11.9	11.8

Question 5

The grid below shows two straight lines representing a road and several points are also displayed.

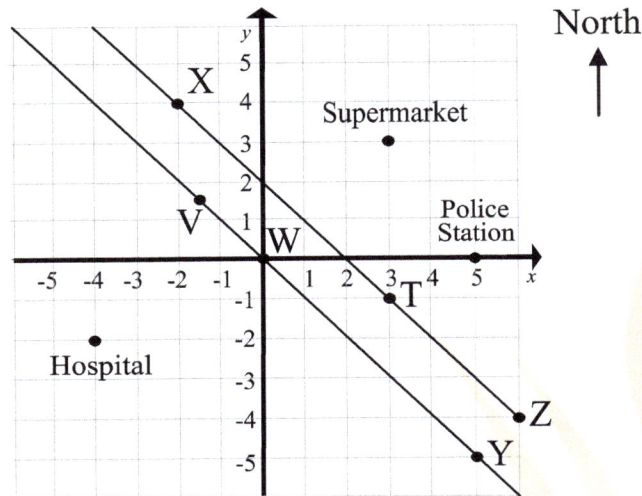

a. Which lettered point is directly west of the police station?

A	B	C	D	E
Y	X	T	Z	W

b. What are the coordinates of the Hospital?

A	B	C	D	E
(-4, -2)	(3, 3)	(-2, -4)	(-2, 4)	(5, 0)

c. If the supermarket is moved 7 units left and 2 units up, then what lettered point on the road will be closest to the supermarket?

A	B	C	D	E
X	T	V	W	Z

d. The police station point is reflected in the line $x = 3$. What are its new coordinates?

A	B	C	D	E
(8, 0)	(1, 0)	(3, 0)	(0, 1)	(0, 0)

e. The distance between points V and Y is 3.75 miles. If 1 mile ≈ 2 km, then what is the approximate distance between the two points in kilometres?

A	B	C	D	E
12.7km	8.7km	7.5km	9km	10.5km

Question 6

The five numbers below represent the first five terms in a number sequence.

-28   -10   8   26   44

a.   What is the highest common factor (HCF) of the third and fifth terms in the number sequence?

A	B	C	D	E
2	44	8	12	4

b.   What is the result of multiplying the first term in the sequence by the second term in the sequence?

A	B	C	D	E
-40	28	-280	-2.8	280

c.   What is the range of the first five terms of the number sequence?

A	B	C	D	E
72	54	5	64	16

d.   What is the sixth term in the number sequence?

A	B	C	D	E
59	26	80	62	74

e.   If Y is added onto the second term in the number sequence and the result is multiplied by 2 to give 10, then what is the value of Y?

A	B	C	D	E
15	10	6	12	17

BLANK PAGE

Test 8

 **20 minutes**

Total

/30

Question 1

Two clock faces are shown below. The clock face on the left shows the time in the morning on Tuesday 9th February and the clock face on the right shows the time on the afternoon of 18th February.

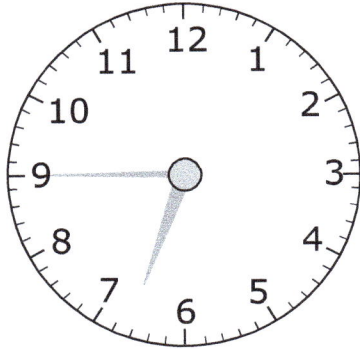

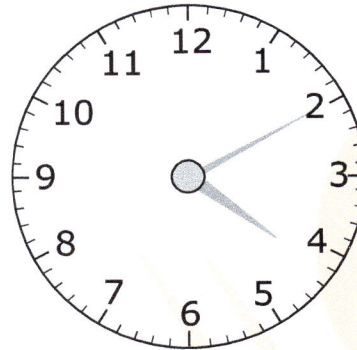

a. Which day of the week will be 18th February?

A	B	C	D	E
Monday	Tuesday	Wednesday	Thursday	Friday

b. What time is shown on the left clock face on 9th February?

A	B	C	D	E
5:50 PM	9:54 AM	6:45 AM	4:10 AM	6:45 PM

c. What time is shown on the right clock face on 18th February in 24 hour clock format?

A	B	C	D	E
16:02	18:45	14:10	14:02	16:10

d. The minute hand on a clock measures 28.5mm in length and the hour hand is 1.96cm in length. How much longer is the minute hand than the hour hand?

A	B	C	D	E
0.93cm	1.11cm	0.89cm	1.03cm	0.98cm

e. The diameter of a clock face is 6.45cm. What is the radius length of a clock face?

A	B	C	D	E
2.6cm	3.5cm	2.25cm	3.08cm	3.225cm

Question 2

Temperatures recorded at 12 noon on six consecutive days are shown on the chart below.

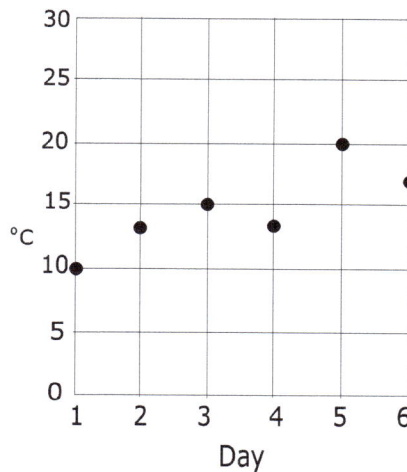

a.   What was the range of temperatures recorded over the six days?

A	B	C	D	E
14°C	20°C	15°C	14.6°C	10°C

b.   What was the mode temperature recorded over the six days?

A	B	C	D	E
13°C	10°C	17°C	20°C	15°C

c.   On which day was the temperature recorded as the value of $\sqrt{400}$°C?

A	B	C	D	E
5	6	1	3	2

d.   By how much was the temperature above minus 22°C on day 1?

A	B	C	D	E
30°C	37°C	32°C	-28°C	22°C

e.   The temperature on the seventh day is an increased of 15% from the temperature seen on the fifth day. What is the temperature on the seventh day?

A	B	C	D	E
27°C	13°C	23°C	25°C	18°C

Question 3

A cuboid money box with height 18cm, length 25cm and width 10cm contains 28 five pence coins, 9 ten pence coins and 3 one pound coins.

a.   How much money in total is in the money box?

A	B	C	D	E
£5.15	£2.33	£5.50	£5.30	£4.95

b.   What is the ratio of five pence coins in the money box to coins of other values in the money box (i.e. ten pence and one pound coins)?

A	B	C	D	E
5:9	7:3	28:9	4:1	28:3

c.   If a coin is selected at random from the money box, what is the probability that it is a five pence coin?

A	B	C	D	E
$\frac{7}{10}$	$\frac{3}{8}$	$\frac{5}{6}$	$\frac{1}{7}$	$\frac{3}{4}$

d.   A quarter of the 5 pence coins are removed from the money box. How many five pence coins are left in the money box?

A	B	C	D	E
20	22	21	18	19

e.   What is the volume of the money box?

A	B	C	D	E
4,800cm^3	4,350cm^3	5,040cm^3	4,500cm^3	4,100cm^3

Question 4

A square and a regular octagon are shown below along with a ruler.

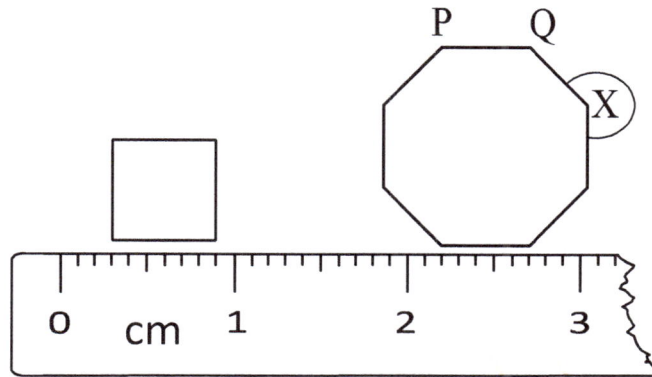

a. What is the size of angle X?

A	B	C	D	E
235°	210°	245°	225°	185°

b. What is the area of the square in mm^2?

A	B	C	D	E
$18mm^2$	$25mm^2$	$36mm^2$	$49mm^2$	$16mm^2$

c. What is the perimeter of the octagon?

A	B	C	D	E
9cm	16cm	8cm	4cm	6cm

d. What is the order of rotational symmetry for a regular octagon?

A	B	C	D	E
2	8	4	6	0

e. How many sides on the octagon are perpendicular to side PQ?

A	B	C	D	E
2	4	1	0	6

Question 5

Carlos has the four values 17, 6, 12 and 8 written down.

a.   What is the lowest common multiple (LCM) of 6, 12 and 8?

A	B	C	D	E
24	48	26	4	180

b.   How many of the four numbers are triangular numbers?

A	B	C	D	E
4	1	3	0	2

c.   Which of the four numbers is the same as $18^0 + \sqrt{49}$?

A	B	C	D	E
4	17	8	12	6

d.   Which one of the four numbers is a prime number?

A	B	C	D	E
6	4	12	8	17

e.   Carlos multiplies 17 by 60 and rounds the result to the nearest 100.
      What should his answer be?

A	B	C	D	E
0	1,000	1,020	1,010	1,100

Question 6

The grid below has five points on it labelled Q, R, S, T and U. The coordinates for a sixth point W are determined using the number machine. The input to the number machine is the x-coordinate of point W and the output to the number machine is the y-coordinate of point W.

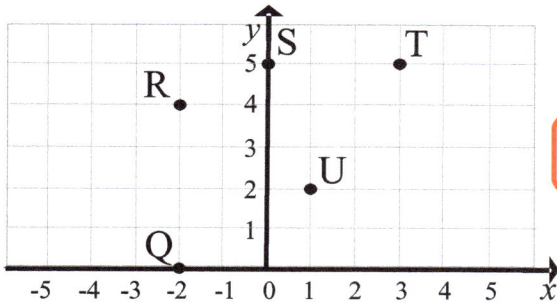

a. What are the coordinates of point S?

A	B	C	D	E
(0, 5)	(-4, 2)	(5, 0)	(3, 4)	(-2, 4)

b. What are the coordinates of point W?

A	B	C	D	E
(3, 4)	(5, 3)	(0, 5)	(4, 2)	(-2, 4)

c. Point Q is rotated 90° clockwise about point (0, 0). What are its new coordinates?

A	B	C	D	E
(2, 2)	(0, 2)	(-2, 0)	(-2, -2)	(0, -2)

d. Point R is translated right 1 unit and down 3 units. What are its new coordinates?

A	B	C	D	E
(1, 3)	(1, -3)	(-3, 1)	(-1, 1)	(1, -4)

e. Point U is reflected in the y-axis. What are its new coordinates?

A	B	C	D	E
(1, -2)	(2, 2)	(1, 2)	(-1, 2)	(2, 0)

BLANK PAGE

Test 9

 **20 minutes**

Total

/30

Question 1

The following net, which when folded up forms a 3D shape, is made up of a square and four identical isosceles triangles.

(Diagram not to scale)

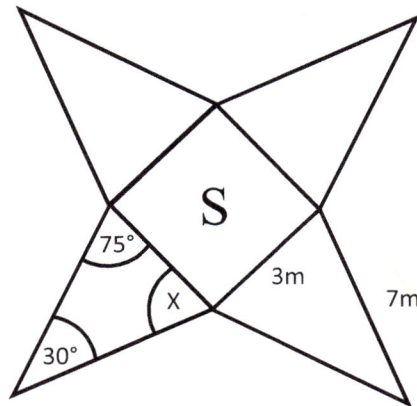

a. What is the area of square S in cm^2?

A	B	C	D	E
30,000cm^2	49,000cm^2	16,000cm^2	90,000cm^2	81,000cm^2

b. What is the perimeter of triangle T?

A	B	C	D	E
17m	16m	10.5m	21m	11m

c. What is the size of angle X?

A	B	C	D	E
75°	60°	85°	30°	45°

d. The area of triangle T is 9.4868m^2. What is the area of triangle T correct to one decimal place?

A	B	C	D	E
9.8m^2	10.0m^2	9.4m^2	9.5m^2	9.0m^2

e. What is the name of the shape that is formed when the net is folded up?

A	B	C	D	E
Tetrahedron	Cylinder	Square based pyramid	Cube	Pentagonal prism

Question 2

The letters of the word PERIMETER are jumbled up and placed into an empty bag. Answer each part which follows assuming that the bag is full of these letters.

a. How many letters in the bag have a horizontal line of symmetry through their centre point?

A	B	C	D	E
6	0	8	4	2

b. If a letter was to be drawn out from the bag at random, then what is the probability of it being an E?

A	B	C	D	E
$^1/_5$	$^2/_7$	$^3/_8$	$^1/_3$	$^3/_{10}$

c. If a letter was to be drawn out from the bag at random then what is the probability of it being an R?

A	B	C	D	E
$^1/_3$	$^1/_9$	$^2/_9$	$^1/_5$	$^2/_5$

d. If two letters were to be drawn out from the bag at random (without replacement), then what is the probability of them being a P followed by an R?

A	B	C	D	E
$^1/_{24}$	$^1/_{36}$	$^2/_{81}$	$^1/_{18}$	$^1/_{72}$

e. What is the ratio of the number of vowels (letters A, E, I, O, U) to the number of non-vowel letters in the bag?

A	B	C	D	E
1:3	5:2	4:9	20:16	4:5

Question 3

Gideon plays a game of throwing six circular rubber hoops onto a board which has various sections worth different points. His results are shown below.

5 points	7 points	10 points	25 points	35 points
○ ○		○	○ ○ ○	

a.   What overall score did Gideon obtain from throwing the six hoops?

A	B	C	D	E
115	95	105	100	97

b.   What was the mode score that Gideon obtained on his throws?

A	B	C	D	E
5	10	25	2	3

c.   What percentage of Gideon's hoops landed in regions worth more than five points?

A	B	C	D	E
50%	100%	75%	80%	66.7%

d.   A circular hoop has a radius of 3.35cm. What is its diameter?

A	B	C	D	E
1.675cm	5.8cm	10.05cm	6.7cm	7.54cm

e.   Gideon has a second game and throws all six of his hoops into the 35 point region on the board. What was his overall score on game 2?

A	B	C	D	E
235	210	180	95	105

Question 4

The number set below consists of eight numbers.

5   19   10   2   23   16   27   4

a. How many of the eight numbers are prime factors of 69?

A	B	C	D	E
3	4	0	1	2

b. What fraction of the eight numbers are prime numbers?

A	B	C	D	E
$^1/_2$	$^3/_8$	$^3/_4$	$^1/_4$	$^1/_8$

c. What percentage of the eight numbers are square numbers?

A	B	C	D	E
40%	37.5%	50%	0%	25%

d. What is the median of the eight numbers?

A	B	C	D	E
23	10	12.5	2	13

e. What is the lowest common multiple (LCM) of 5, 10 and 16?

A	B	C	D	E
100	5	1	80	160

Question 5

Biyu leaves home one morning at 10:15. She completes the table of tasks below in order, one after the other without having a break between tasks.

List of tasks and duration

Task	Duration
Walk to town	38 minutes
Have breakfast	40 minutes
Shop	1.8 hours
Have a coffee	15 minutes
Bus ride home	18 minutes

a. How long does Biyu shop for in minutes?

A	B	C	D	E
218 min	106 min	180 min	184 min	108 min

b. What time does Biyu finish having breakfast?

A	B	C	D	E
11:17 AM	10:53AM	12:16 PM	10:55 AM	11:33 AM

c. The shopping costs £127.33. Biyu pays for the shopping using three fifty pound notes. How much change will she receive?

A	B	C	D	E
£24.67	£47.67	£22.67	£18.33	£17.67

d. The shopping weighed 4.5 kilograms (kg) in total. If 1 ounce (oz) ≈ 25 grams (g), then how many ounces did the shopping approximately weigh?

A	B	C	D	E
145 oz	180 oz	112.5 oz	165 oz	100 oz

e. Biyu spent 5.2 minutes walking from the bus stop to her home. How long was her walk in seconds?

A	B	C	D	E
320 seconds	300 seconds	318 seconds	360 seconds	312 seconds

Question 6

The first five terms of a number sequence are shown on the chart below.

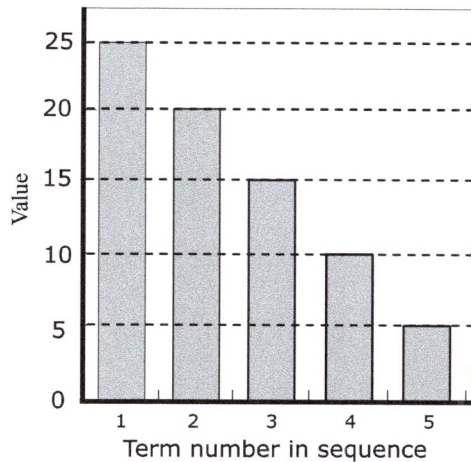

a. What is the sum of the first five terms in the number sequence?

A	B	C	D	E
95	65	57	80	75

b. What percentage of the first five terms in the number sequence are odd numbers that are greater than or equal to 10?

A	B	C	D	E
0%	40%	20%	80%	60%

c. What is the sixth term in the number sequence?

A	B	C	D	E
0	4	10	-5	15

d. What is the seventh term in the number sequence?

A	B	C	D	E
3	10	-5	0	-10

e. If the first term in the number sequence is divided by a number X, the result is 12.25. What is the value of X?

A	B	C	D	E
5	10	7	2	3

BLANK PAGE

Test 10

 **20 minutes**

Total

/30

Question 1

£120 is planned to be split three ways between Hayley, David and Sam in the ratio of 13:2:5.

a.   How much money should Hayley receive?

A	B	C	D	E
£58	£76	£75	£82	£78

b.   How much more money should Sam receive than David?

A	B	C	D	E
£9	£12	£42	£18	£30

c.   If Hayley was to instead receive 70% of the £120, then how much money would she receive?

A	B	C	D	E
£84	£96	£50	£79	£70

d.   If Sam was to instead receive £24, then what fraction of the £120 will he receive?

A	B	C	D	E
$\frac{1}{4}$	$\frac{1}{6}$	$\frac{1}{3}$	$\frac{6}{24}$	$\frac{1}{5}$

e.   David actually receives £55.28 of the £120 and puts it in the bank. Before receiving this money he had £Y in the bank. After receiving this money he had £924.75 in the bank. What was the value of Y?

A	B	C	D	E
£896.56	£869.75	£869.47	£869.74	£796.74

Question 2

The grid below show a rectangle and also a circle with centre point X. The units for the axes are in centimetres.

(Diagram not to scale)

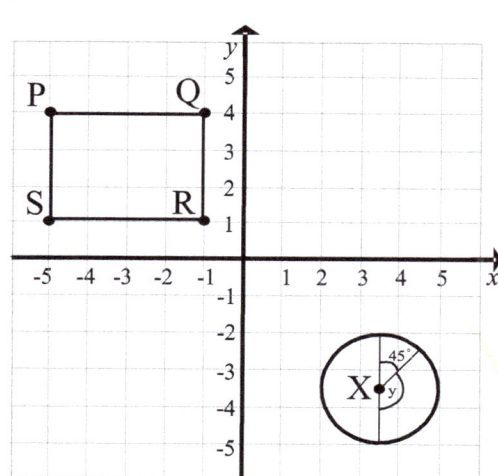

a. What is the size of angle y?

A	B	C	D	E
135°	155°	315°	138°	145°

b. What is the radius length of the circle?

A	B	C	D	E
2cm	3cm	1cm	1.5cm	4.5cm

c. What are the coordinates of point P?

A	B	C	D	E
(-5, 4)	(3.5, -3.5)	(-1, 1)	(-5, 1)	(4, -5)

d. What is the perimeter of the rectangle?

A	B	C	D	E
12cm	14cm	8cm	2cm	16cm

e. If the rectangle is translated 3 units down and 1 unit left then what are the new coordinates of point R?

A	B	C	D	E
(2, 0)	(4, -2)	(-3, 1)	(-2, -2)	(2, -2)

Question 3

Two scales are shown below and are labelled 1 and 2.

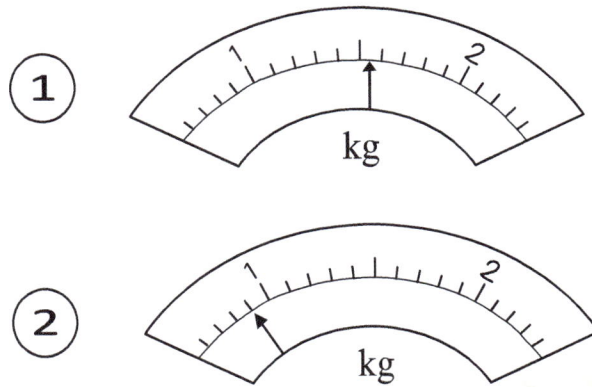

a.   What weight is shown on the first set of scales?

A	B	C	D	E
1.65kg	1.34kg	1.50kg	1.45kg	1.55kg

b.   How much is the weight shown on the second set of scales less than 2,000g?

A	B	C	D	E
720g	450g	900g	1,100g	590g

c.   A third set of scales shows a weight of 6,398g. What is this weight in kilograms correct to one decimal place?

A	B	C	D	E
6.0kg	7.0kg	6.4kg	6.3kg	6.8kg

d.   A fourth set of scales shows a weight of 15kg. If 14 pounds (lbs) ≈ 6kg then how many pounds is 15kg?

A	B	C	D	E
34lbs	29lbs	7lbs	21lbs	35lbs

e.   A fifth set of scales shows a weight of (5 × 5 × 5) grams. What is this in index form?

A	B	C	D	E
3^5g	5^3g	15g	25g	125g

Question 4

The first seven terms of a number sequence are shown below.

0   3   5   6   10   12   15

a. What is the range of the first seven terms of the number sequence?

A	B	C	D	E
1	0	15	14	6

b. What is the probability that the eighth term in the sequence is 7?

A	B	C	D	E
$\frac{1}{2}$	$\frac{1}{3}$	1	0	$\frac{7}{8}$

c. What is the ninth term in the number sequence?

A	B	C	D	E
25	15	24	18	20

d. How many of the first seven terms of the number sequence are triangular numbers?

A	B	C	D	E
0	4	5	6	2

e. How many of terms 2 to 6 in the number sequence are factors of 36 and 60?

A	B	C	D	E
1	5	0	3	2

Question 5

Andrew records the number of cars each household owns down a small road. His findings are shown in the tally table below.

Number of cars	Tally	Frequency
0	⦀⦀⦀⦀ ⦀⦀⦀⦀ |||	13
1	⦀⦀⦀⦀ ||||	9
2	⦀⦀⦀⦀	5
3	|||	?

a. How many households own three cars?

A	B	C	D	E
4	3	13	0	5

b. How many cars were owned on this particular road?

A	B	C	D	E
33	45	41	30	28

c. What fraction of households owned at least one car?

A	B	C	D	E
$3/10$	$17/30$	$17/41$	$17/28$	$1/3$

d. What was the median number of cars owned per household?

A	B	C	D	E
3	2	1	0	13

e. What was the mode number of cars owned per household?

A	B	C	D	E
0	2	3	1	13

Question 6

A cuboid and a tetrahedron are shown below.

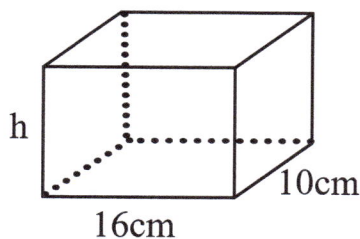

(Diagram not to scale)

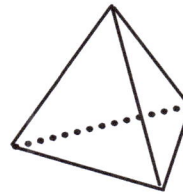

h

16cm

10cm

Volume = 1280cm^3

Volume = 960cm^3

a. What is the height of the cuboid labelled h?

A	B	C	D	E
1.6cm	10cm	16cm	8cm	4cm

b. How much larger is the volume of the cuboid than the volume of the tetrahedron?

A	B	C	D	E
340cm^3	320cm^3	300cm^3	280cm^3	360cm^3

c. How many vertices would nine cuboids have in total?

A	B	C	D	E
108	72	81	90	85

d. How many total edges are on eight tetrahedrons?

A	B	C	D	E
48	36	32	28	46

e. What is the total combined volume of two identical cuboids and three identical tetrahedrons basing both objects on those shown in the diagram above?

A	B	C	D	E
5,760cm^3	5,100cm^3	5,440cm^3	5,840cm^3	6,400cm^3

BLANK PAGE

FIRST PAST THE POST®

Answers & Explanations

Numerical Reasoning:
Multi-Part

Multiple Choice
Book 2

Question	Answer		Explanation
1a	B	£158	£127 + £84 - £53 = £211 - £53 = **£158**.
1b	E	£157	The bracket means that £84 - £53 is calculated first and then the result added to £127, giving the part 1a answer of £158. Finally, £158 - £1 = **£157**.
1c	A	7.5cm	1.5 × 50cm = 75cm, 75cm ÷ 10 = **7.5cm**.
1d	E	15cm	Halving the divisor of 10 gives a divisor of 5. 1.5 × 50cm = 75cm, 75cm ÷ 5 = **15cm**.
1e	C	97	Due to the presence of different operations in this sum, BIDMAS must be considered. Solve bracketed sum first and note that (÷) comes before (+): (96 ÷ 12 + 3) = 8 + 3 = 11. Next, (×) comes before (-): 12 × 11 = 132. Finally, 132 - 35 = **97**.
2a	B	2	The parallelogram, shape P, maps onto itself twice when rotated through 360° and therefore has an order of rotational symmetry of **2**.
2b	D	6cm^2	As Shape P covers an area of six small grid squares, area = 6 × 1cm^2 = **6cm^2**.
2c	D	45°	As the two shorter sides of triangle R are the same length, it is an isosceles triangle. The sum of the two smaller angles must be 90°. Therefore, angle S = 90° ÷ 2 = **45°**.
2d	A	(-2, -3)	The third corner of the isosceles triangle must have a y-coordinate value at the centre of the base line TU, i.e. at -3. The only option available is **(-2, -3)**.
2e	E	(1, -2)	As line L slants at an angle of 45°, rotating line L 90° anticlockwise about point (3, -4) moves the end of the line V to **(1, -2)**.
3a	C	$^5/_8$	Each term is produced by adding $^1/_8$ to the previous term. Therefore, missing term S is given by $(^1/_2) + (^1/_8) = (^4/_8) + (^1/_8) = $**$^5/_8$**.
3b	C	$^9/_8$	$(^3/_8) + (^3/_4) = (^3/_8) + (^6/_8) = $**$^9/_8$**.
3c	E	20	The number of rows and the number of columns each increase by one with each term. As term 3 has 3 rows × 4 columns, term 4 must have 4 rows × 5 columns = **20** smiley faces.
3d	B	6	The sequence consists of ascending prime numbers, so missing term T is 2. The LCM of 2 and 3 is **6**.
3e	D	1 and 19	Missing term U is 19, because it is the next prime number after 17. All prime numbers have only two factors, **1** and the number itself, **19**.

Question		Answer	Explanation
4a	E	× 9	Working from the input: 12 ÷ 4 = 3. Of the five options given, only 3 × **9** gives an output of 27.
4b	A	4:9	Input of number machine 1 = 12. Output of number machine 1 = 27. Therefore, the ratio is 12:27 or **4:9**.
4c	C	80	Working from the output and applying inverse operations: (27 - 7) × 4 = 20 × 4 = **80**.
4d	D	15	Working from the input: 1.5 × 6 = 9, 9 - 12 = -3, -3 + 18 = **15**.
4e	D	5 tenths	Input of number machine 2 = 1.5. The 5 is in the tenths column and is therefore worth **5 tenths**.
5a	B	24	Number of red cars sold (9) + number of blue cars sold (15) = **24**.
5b	B	5	Silver cars sold = 27, black cars sold = 22, difference = 27 - 22 = **5**.
5c	C	92	Total = 27 + 19 + 9 + 22 + 15 = **92** cars sold.
5d	E	33	Black cars sold during original 6 months = 22. 50% of 22 = $(^{50}/_{100})$ × 22 = 100% of 22 + 50% of 22 = 22 + 11 = **33**.
5e	D	2,580kg	Total tonnage = 1.08 + 1.5 = 2.58 tonnes. As 1 tonne = 1,000kg, 2.58 tonnes × 1000 = **2,580kg**.
6a	C	300°	Interior angles of an equilateral triangle are 60°. Angle S = 360° - 60° = **300°**.
6b	A	4 triangles, 1 square	The pyramid shown is square-based. It therefore requires **1 square** to form the base and **4 triangles** to form the sides when folded up.
6c	A	2	Number of faces = 5, number of vertices = 5, number of edges = 8. Therefore, 5 + 5 - 8 = 10 - 8 = **2**.
6d	E	5,400cm^2	Area of box base = 90cm × 60cm = **5,400cm^2**.
6e	B	96	As the base of the large box measures 90cm × 60cm, and the small cube width is 15cm, 90 ÷ 15 (6 cubes) by 60 ÷ 15 (4 cubes) = 24 cubes. This is the maximum number that can be packed in one layer. Four such layers will fill the 60cm high box. Therefore, 4 × 24 = **96**.

Question		Answer	Explanation
1a	D	0.02	As each large division is worth 0.1, so one small division is worth $0.1 \div 5 = $ **0.02**.
1b	C	3.77	The arrow is pointing to a value of 3.7 plus 3.5 small divisions, each worth 0.02. $3.7 + (3.5 \times 0.02) = 3.7 + 0.07 = $ **3.77**.
1c	C	$^6/_{10}$	The 6 in 3.6 is in the tenths column and is worth 6 tenths or $^6/_{10}$.
1d	A	900ml	1L = 1,000ml The reading on the jug scale indicates 0.9 litres of water. 0.9 litres × 1000 = **900ml**
1e	E	6	Number of full glasses = 900ml ÷ 150ml = **6**.
2a	D	72°	Kettle angle = 360° - (90° + 108° + 36° + 54°) = 360° - 288° = **72°**.
2b	A	12	The angle representing the number of printers sold is 54° which is equivalent to six items sold. The angle representing the number of phones sold is 108° which is double that of the printer. Therefore, number of phones sold = 6 × 2 = **12**
2c	B	10%	The angle representing the number of watches sold is 36° from a total of the available 360°. As a percentage: $^{36}/_{360} \times 100\% = $ **10%**
2d	E	8	Mean = sum of terms ÷ number of terms in set Sum of terms= 8 + 6 + 12 + 4 + 10 = 40 Mean = 40 ÷ 5 = **8**.
2e	E	8^2	To find the median, the five sales figures must be reordered in ascending numerical order: 4, 6, **8**, 10, 12. The middle figure 8 is the median. Range = 12 - 4 = 8. Therefore, the product is 8 × 8, or **8^2**.
3a	B	$^1/_2$	1, 4, 49 and 64 are square numbers. P(square) = $^4/_8 = $ **$^1/_2$**.
3b	D	$^1/_4$	There are two triangular numbers on the number grid: 1 and 15. P(triangular) = $^2/_8 = $ **$^1/_4$**.
3c	D	14 and 15	Consecutive numbers follow on in order: **14 and 15**.
3d	A	NE	A prime number has only two factors: 1 and the number itself. Note: 1 is not a prime number Therefore, the only number in the grid which is prime is 7. Jill must therefore walk Northeast (**NE**).
3e	C	$^3/_8$	1, 27 and 64 are cube numbers. P(cube) = **$^3/_8$**.

Question		Answer	Explanation
4a	E	6(r + s)	Perimeter (P) = 4r + 2r + 3s + s + 2s = 6r + 6s = **6(r + s)**.
4b	C	2cm	From part 4 (a), P = 6(r + s). Therefore, 30cm = 6(3cm + s), 30 ÷ 6 = 3 + s, 5 = 3 + s, 5 - 3 = s, s = **2cm**.
4c	C	Irregular Pentagon	Shape 1a has five sides of different lengths and is therefore an **irregular pentagon**.
4d	A	8cm	Length LK = 4s, where s = 2cm (from part 4(b)). Therefore, LK = 4 × 2cm = **8cm**.
4e	D	16cm^2	Perpendicular height of triangle = 2s = 2 × 2cm = 4cm. Area = $^1/_2$ × b × h = $^1/_2$ × 8cm × 4cm = **16cm^2**.
5a	E	20	Train 2 leaves Cantlow at 08:48 and arrives in Highlong at 09:08. The time difference between 08:48 and 09:08 is **20 minutes**.
5b	B	08:33	As train 1 does not stop at Fulwood, Ryan must catch train 2 from Oakdale at **08:33**.
5c	A	20:23	Although train 3 and train 4 are returning trains from Langley to Oakdale, only train 4 covers the journey from Langley to Bandford in exactly 24 minutes. Train 4 departs from Langley at **20:23**.
5d	C	£19.50	Total cost = (£7.80 × 2) + £7.80 ÷ 2 = £15.60 + £3.90 = **£19.50**.
5e	D	360	The time difference between Fulwood and Bandford for train 4 is 6 minutes. 6 × 60 = **360** seconds
6a	A	(0, 4)	The x-coordinate of point P is 0 and its y-coordinate is 4: **(0, 4)**.
6b	D	(4, 0)	Rotating point P 90° clockwise about (0, 0) brings P to **(4, 0)**.
6c	D	(3.5, 4.5)	The coordinates of the upper end of line L are (2, 6) and the coordinates of the lower end are (5, 3). The x-coordinate at the centre of the line is (2 + 5) ÷ 2 = 3.5. The y-coordinate at the centre of the line is (6 + 3) ÷ 2 = 4.5. Therefore, the coordinates of the centre of the line are **(3.5, 4.5)**.
6d	B	(8, 5)	The mirror image of the square S appears the same distance above the mirror line as it is below it. This puts corner Z at coordinates **(8, 5)**.
6e	B	8	The square S has 4 lines of symmetry. It also maps onto itself 4 times when rotated through 360°. Therefore, its order of rotational symmetry is 4. 4 + 4 = **8**.

Question		Answer	Explanation
1a	B	$^3/_4$	As the term before T is 1, T = (1 + 2) ÷ 4 = $^3/_4$.
1b	C	38	Working backwards through the rule from term 2, S = (10 × 4) - 2 = **38**.
1c	E	30	Multiples of 10 are 10, 20, 30, 40... and multiples of 6 are 6, 12, 18, 24, 30, 36... Lowest common multiple (LCM) of 10 and 6 is therefore **30**.
1d	E	50%	Three of the six terms, 1, 6 and 10, are triangular numbers. $^3/_6 \times 100$ = **50%**
1e	D	Term 4	A prime number has only two factors: 1 and the number itself. Note: 1 is not a prime number. The only prime number in the sequence is 2 i.e. **Term 4**.
2a	A	24cm	One side of a single small equilateral triangle = 12cm ÷ 3 = 4cm. One side of the large outer equilateral triangle = 2 × 4cm = 8cm. Perimeter of large outer equilateral triangle = 3 × 8cm = **24cm**.
2b	D	120°	Each of the three interior angles of an equilateral triangle are equal to 60°. Therefore, angle P = 2 × 60° = **120°**.
2c	D	Regular Tetrahedron	As Shape 1 is a pyramid made up of four identical equilateral triangles, it is called a **Regular Tetrahedron**.
2d	C	77cm³	Volume = end area × height = 11cm² × 7cm = **77cm³**.
2e	B	18	Shape 2 has 12 end edges (6 at the top, 6 at the bottom), and 6 edges around its sides. Total = 12 + 6 = **18**.
3a	E	50	Survey number = 14 + 12 + 10 + 5 + 4 + 3 + 2 = **50**.
3b	C	23	Number of children that eat pizza = 12 + 5 + 4 + 2 = **23**.
3c	A	2:5	Number of children that eat fish = 10 + 5 + 3 + 2 = 20. Ratio is 20:50 which reduces down to **2:5**.
3d	A	14	Observe number in main area of bottom circle (non-overlapping region) which is **14**.
3e	D	2	Central area number **2**.

Test 3, pages 17-24

Question	Answer		Explanation
4a	D	1.12m	9cm = 9cm ÷ 100 = 0.09m Riya's height = 1.21m - 0.09m = **1.12m**.
4b	E	1,210mm	To convert metres (m) into millimetres (mm) multiply by 1000, 1.21 × 1000 = **1,210mm**.
4c	B	2.4kg	As each small scale division represents 0.4kg, 3 tins have a mass of 2kg + 0.4kg = **2.4kg**.
4d	C	800g	Three tins have a mass of 2.4kg = 2,400g. Mass of one tin = 2,400g ÷ 3 = **800g**.
4e	C	16kg	One tin has a mass of 800g, so 20 tins have a mass of 2 × 10 x 800g = 2 × 8,000g = 16,000g. 16,000g ÷ 1000 = **16kg**.
5a	D	Subtract $4x$ from both sides	Looking at the x terms only, **subtracting $4x$ from both sides** creates $4x - 4x$ on the right which gives 0, and $8x - 4x$ on the left, which has achieved the aim.
5b	A	4	$8x - 7 = 4x + 9 \rightarrow$ subtract $4x$ from both sides: $8x - 4x - 7 = 4x - 4x + 9 \rightarrow 4x - 7 = 9$ Add 7 to both sides: $4x - 7 + 7 = 9 + 7 \rightarrow 4x = 16$ Divide both sides by 4: $4x ÷ 4 = 16 ÷ 4 \rightarrow x = $ **4**.
5c	E	$5n$	Left side of equation is $3n + 2n = $ **$5n$**.
5d	B	$n = pt/5$	$3n + 2n = pt \rightarrow 5n = pt \rightarrow$ divide both sides by 5: $5n/5 = pt/5 \rightarrow n = $ **$pt/5$**.
5e	C	57	Substituting numbers in $(a + 9b)(2c - 3a)$ gives $(1 + 18)(6 - 3) = 19 × 3 = $ **57**.
6a	C	5	Mean score = sum of scores ÷ number of scores $6 = (12 + 2 + N + 10 + 3 + 2 + 8) ÷ 7 \rightarrow 6 = (37 + N) ÷ 7 \rightarrow 6 × 7 = 37 + N \rightarrow$ $42 = 37 + N \rightarrow 42 - 37 = N \rightarrow N = $ **5**.
6b	E	2	The mode is the score that occurs most often. This is the number **2**.
6c	A	5	Scores in order are: 2, 2, 3, 5, 8, 10, 12. The median is the centre score, **5**.
6d	A	10	The highest score is 12 and the lowest score is 2. Range = 12 - 2 = **10**.
6e	D	$^1/_3$	There are two odd numbers on the spinner, namely, 3 and 5. Therefore, P(odd) = $^2/_6$ = **$^1/_3$**.

Test 4, pages 25-32

Question	Answer		Explanation
1a	D	400	Output = input ÷ 0.25 = 100 ÷ 0.25 = 10,000 ÷ 25 = **400**.
1b	E	25	Working backwards from the output and applying inverse operations: Input = 100 × 0.25 = **25**.
1c	A	6x - 2 = 28	Basic equation format is: Input (instruction 1) (instruction 2) = output. x(× 6)(- 2) = 28. This gives **6x - 2 = 28**.
1d	C	5	Working backwards from the output and reversing signs gives (28 + 2) ÷ 6 = 30 ÷ 6 = 5. Or, using the formula in 1c, 6x - 2 = 28 → 6x = 28 + 2 → x = 30 ÷ 6 = **5**.
1e	C	0	Working from the input, the output of the first box is 5 + 15 = 20. Next, the output of the second box is 20 ÷ 0.5 = 40. Finally, the output of the third box is 40 × 0 = 0. Therefore, the output is **0**.
2a	C	(2, 3)	From the origin (0, 0), the Aquarium is 2 units right the x-axis and 3 units up. Hence the x-value is 2 and the y-value is 3. Therefore, the coordinates are **(2, 3)**.
2b	D	NW	As north is shown vertically up, the Aquarium is Northwest (**NW**) of the ship.
2c	A	SW	As north is shown vertically up, the Pier is Southwest (**SW**) of the Aquarium.
2d	C	(5, 4)	The x-value of corner C can be observed directly as **5**. Side length of the square can be obtained from the known x-values at the top i.e. 8 - 5 = 3. Therefore, y-value at corner C = 7 - 3 = **4**. Therefore, the coordinates of C are (**5, 4**).
2e	E	(2, 3)	Three units to the left moves the corner C x-value to 5 - 3 = **2**. One unit down moves the corner C y-value to 4 - 1 = **3**, Coordinates of C are (**2, 3**).
3a	A	14	From Table 2, a 15 - 16 size pullover costs £9. From Table 1, 15 - 16 requires **14** 50g balls.
3b	D	£37.50	From Table 2, a 12 - 14 size pullover costs £7.50. The cost for five = 5 × £7.50 = **£37.50**.
3c	A	6 - 8	From Table 2, £12.50 (one adult size) + £6.00 (one 9 - 11 size) = £18.50, Cost of third pullover = £23.00 - £18.50 = £4.50 which corresponds to size **6 - 8** years.
3d	E	22	From Table 1, 2 × 8 (two adult size) + 1 × 6 (one 12 - 14 size) = 16 + 6 = **22** 100g balls.
3e	B	50	1kg = 1,000g 30kg = 30,000g so the number of 100g balls = 30,000g ÷ 100g = 300, From Table 1, six (100g) balls make a 12 - 14 size pullover, no. of pullovers = 300 ÷ 6 = **50**.

Question	Answer		Explanation
4a	E	Irregular Octagon	Shape has 8 sides of different lengths so is therefore an **Irregular Octagon**.
4b	B	10cm	Perimeter = 3cm + 2cm + 3cm + 2cm = 6cm + 4cm = **10cm**.
4c	A	12cm²	Area of shaded rectangles = length × width = 6cm × 2cm = **12cm²**.
4d	C	Triangular Prism	Shape 2 has two identical triangular ends parallel to each other and is therefore termed a **Triangular Prism**.
4e	C	120cm³	Volume = one end area × prism length = 10cm² × 12cm = **120cm³**.
5a	E	$^2/_3$	For the score to be greater than 2, it must be a 3, 4, 5 or 6. Therefore, P(>2) = $^4/_6$ = $\mathbf{^2/_3}$.
5b	B	$^1/_2$	There are three prime numbers available, namely, 2, 3 and 5. P(prime) = $^3/_6$ = $\mathbf{^1/_2}$.
5c	E	$^1/_{36}$	On first roll, P(3) = $^1/_6$. On second roll, P(3) = $^1/_6$. P(3 twice) = $(^1/_6) \times (^1/_6)$ = $\mathbf{^1/_{36}}$.
5d	D	$^1/_{16}$	With the four cards removed, cards left in pack = 52 - 4 = 48 and number of Aces left in the pack is 3 as one was removed. Therefore, P(Ace) = $^3/_{48}$ = $\mathbf{^1/_{16}}$.
5e	C	$^1/_2$	The five and queen are from the black suit of clubs, P(black suit) = $^2/_4$ = $\mathbf{^1/_2}$.
6a	B	42	Sum of ratio parts = 7 + 9 = 16. One part = 96 ÷ 16 = 6, Number of blue counters = 7 × 6 = **42**.
6b	C	12	Number of red counters = 96 - 42 = 54, or 9 × 6 = 54. Difference between red and blue numbers = 54 - 42 = **12**.
6c	E	$^9/_{16}$	Fraction of counters that are red = $^{54}/_{96}$ which can be reduced down to $^9/_{16}$, by dividing through by 6.
6d	A	43.75%	Percentage of counters that are blue = $(^{42}/_{96}) \times 100$ = $(^7/_{16}) \times 100$ = $(^7/_4) \times 25$ = $^{175}/_4$ = **43.75%**.
6e	A	6 units	The 6 in the number 96 is in the units column and therefore worth **6 units**.

Test 5, pages 33-40

Question	Answer		Explanation
1a	A	42cm	The square has a perimeter of 168cm, so the length of one of its sides is 168 ÷ 4 = **42cm**.
1b	C	2	The shape has **2** lines of symmetry.
1c	C	21cm	The square has side length 42cm. Therefore, the equilateral triangles have a base length **21cm**, which is the length of X.
1d	B	1764cm^2	The square has a side length 42cm. The area of the square is 42cm × 42cm = **1764cm^2**.
1e	E	1800cm^2	1764cm^2 rounded to the nearest 100 is **1800cm^2**.
2a	E	$^3/_8$	$^{36}/_{96}$ can be written as $^3/_8$ when divided through by 12.
2b	D	$^5/_6$	$^5/_6$ = 0.83 is the closest of the six fractions to 1.
2c	A	$^{19}/_{12}$	Two largest valued fractions from given set: $^5/_6$ and $^3/_4$. To sum them, they must have a common denominator. LCM of 6 and 4: 12 (new common denominator). $^5/_6 + {}^3/_4 = {}^{10}/_{12} + {}^9/_{12} = \mathbf{{}^{19}/_{12}}$.
2d	D	36	The smallest valued fraction in the given set is $^1/_3$. $^1/_3 × 108 = \mathbf{36}$
2e	B	$^1/_2$	$1\,^3/_4 - 1\,^1/_4 = {}^7/_4 - {}^5/_4 = {}^2/_4 = \mathbf{{}^1/_2}$
3a	A	8.54	Working from the input, the output of the first box is 2.65 + 3.37 = 6.02. The output from the second box is 6.02 × 2 = 12.04. The output from the third box is 12.04 - 3.5 = 8.54. Therefore, the output is **8.541**.
3b	D	3	2.65 rounded to the nearest whole number is **3**.
3c	C	26	Working from the input, the output of the first box is -27 + 4^3 = -27 + 64 = 37. The output of the second box is 37 - √121 = 37 - 11 = 26. Therefore, the output is **26**.
3d	E	13	The highest common factor (HCF) of 39 and 26 is **13**.
3e	A	-24.3	90% of -27 = $^{90}/_{100}$ × -27 = **-24.3**.

Question		Answer	Explanation
4a	A	50cm	If we convert all terms in the number sequence to cm, then we have, 50cm, 100cm, 150cm, 200cm. The difference between each term is **50cm**.
4b	E	125cm	Mean = sum of terms ÷ number of terms Sum of terms = 50 + 100 + 150 + 200 = 500 Mean = 500 ÷ 4 = **125cm**.
4c	D	1:3	The first term is 50cm and the third term 150cm, so the ratio is 50:150 = **1:3**.
4d	B	0.0025km	The next term in the sequence is 200cm + 50cm = 250cm. 250cm = 2.5m = **0.0025km**.
4e	C	1.75m	1m + Y = 2.75m Y = 2.75m - 1m = **1.75m**
5a	C	2cm	The volume of four identical cubes is $32,000mm^3$. Hence, the volume of one of the cubes is $32,000 ÷ 4 = 8,000mm^3$. A cube must have equal length, height and width, so as $8,000 = 20 × 20 × 20$ the length of one side of the cube is 20mm, which is **2cm**.
5b	D	24	One square based pyramid has 8 edges, so three have $3 × 8 =$ **24 edges**.
5c	C	$^1/_3$	There are five pentagonal prisms out of the 15 shapes. Therefore, the probability of selecting one at random would be $^5/_{15} = $ **$^1/_3$**.
5d	E	$^4/_5$	The cylinders have 3 faces each, the cubes 6 faces each, pentagonal prisms 7 faces each and the square based pyramids 5 faces each. Therefore, 12 of the 15 shapes have 4 or more faces, which is $^{12}/_{15} = $ **$^4/_5$**.
5e	A	50	One pentagonal prism has 10 vertices, so five have $10 × 5 = $ **50 vertices**.
6a	A	(-5, 2)	From the origin, point U is 5 units left and 2 units up. Hence, the x-value is -5 and the y-value is 2. Therefore, the coordinates of Point U is **(-5, 2)**.
6b	D	(1, 3)	Point R is at coordinates (-1, 3). If it is reflected in the y-axis then point R would be at coordinates **(1, 3)**.
6c	B	T	Five units to the right moves the x-value to -4 + 5 = 1. Three units down moves the y-value to -1 - 3 = -4 This gives the coordinates of (1,-4). Therefore, the point which is at the coordinates (1, -4) is Point **T**.
6d	C	(-3, -2)	Point Q is at coordinates (3, 2). If it is rotated 180° clockwise about point (0, 0) then its new coordinates would be **(-3, -2)**.
6e	D	P	Point **P** at coordinates (1, 5) is directly North of given coordinates (1, 4).

Test 6, pages 41-48

Question	Answer		Explanation
1a	A	6cm^2	The top of the trapezium is 22cm and the bottom is 16cm. Therefore, the top is 22 - 16 = 6cm longer than the bottom, which means the base of each triangle is 6cm ÷ 2 = 3cm. Area of the triangle T1 is = $^1/_2$ × base × height = $^1/_2$ × 3 × 4 = **6cm^2**.
1b	B	64cm^2	The area of rectangle R = length × height = 16cm × 4cm = **64cm^2**.
1c	D	76cm^2	The area of the trapezium is the areas of R + T1 + T2 = 64cm^2 + 6cm^2 + 6cm^2 = **76cm^2**.
1d	B	48cm	The perimeter of the trapezium is 22cm + 5cm + 16cm + 5cm = **48cm**.
1e	E	2,880m	The actual scaled perimeter of the swimming pool in metres is 0.48 × 6,000 = **2,880m**.
2a	B	5	**5** of the 8 pages had more than 2 spelling errors on them.
2b	C	3	To find the median we have to list the number of spelling errors in ascending numerical order. This is 1, 1, 2, 3, 3, 4, 5, 5. The median of the 8 terms is half way between the fourth and fifth term, which is **3**.
2c	D	25%	2 of the 8 pages had 1 spelling error on them = $^2/_8$ × 100 = $^1/_4$ × 100 = **25%**.
2d	D	3	Mean = sum of terms ÷ number of terms. Sum of spelling errors on all pages = 1 + 5 + 2 + 1 + 3 + 3 + 4 + 5 = 24. Number of pages = 3. Mean = 24 ÷ 8 = **3**
2e	A	$^1/_2$	4 of the 8 pages in the leaflet had between 2 and 4 spelling errors on them = $^4/_8$ = $^1/_2$.
3a	D	£80	12 DVDs cost £4.50 each and 8 CDs cost £3.25 each. Therefore (12 × £4.50) + (8 × £3.25) = £54 + £26 = **£80** was spent in total on the DVDs and CDs.
3b	E	3:2	The ratio of DVDs to CDs is 12:8 = **3:2**.
3c	A	50%	The running time of the DVD is 3 hours = 3 × 60 = 180 minutes. The film is 90 minutes in length = $^{90}/_{180}$ × 100 = **50%** of the playing time of the DVD.
3d	B	37.685cm	Since the question asks for 37.6847cm to be rounded to three decimal places, the fourth decimal place must be considered. As 7 is greater than or equal to 5, the digit in the third decimal place must be rounded up. Therefore, 37.6847cm is **37.685cm** rounded to three decimal places.
3e	A	1.97cm	10mm = 1cm so 99mm = 9.9cm. 11.87cm - 9.9cm = **1.97cm**.

Test 6, pages 41-48

Question	Answer		Explanation
4a	D	54 mins	The time between leaving Hammersmith at 14:44 and arriving at Barking at 15:38 is **54 minutes**.
4b	C	14:59	14:44 + 15 minutes = **14:59**.
4c	E	3:14 PM	15:14 in 12-hour format can be found by subtracting 12 from the hour. This gives **3:14 PM**. PM is written to indicate that it is the afternoon.
4d	B	15 min	900 sec is 900 ÷ 60 = **15 min**.
4e	A	$^3/_{10}$	$^1/_2 - {}^1/_5 = ({}^1/_2 \times {}^5/_5) - ({}^1/_5 \times {}^2/_2) = {}^5/_{10} - {}^2/_{10} = \mathbf{{}^3/_{10}}$.
5a	A	40	The range of terms is the largest value - the smallest value = 40.5 - 0.5 = **40**.
5b	A	121.5	Each term in the number sequence is obtained by multiplying the previous term by 3. Therefore, the sixth term is 40.5 × 3 = **121.5**.
5c	D	3	Lets call the number Amit thinks of Y. He multiplies it by 3 and adds 4.5 to the result to get 13.5. Hence, 3Y + 4.5 = 13.5. Subtracting 4.5 from both sides gives 3Y = 13.5 - 4.5. Therefore, 3Y = 9 and dividing both sides by 3 gives Y = 9 ÷ 3 = **3**.
5d	C	0	Anything multiplied by 0 is 0. This means the 1,800th term multiplied by 0 is **0**.
5e	C	0.75	0.5 is **0.75** above - 0.25.
6a	E	15cm	Volume = length × breadth × height. Therefore, 300 = l × 2 × 10 and l = 300 ÷ (2 × 10) = 300 ÷ 20 = **15cm**.
6b	C	0.33 feet	As 1 inch ≈ 2.5cm, the height of the cuboid, 10cm is approximately 10 ÷ 2.5 = 4 inches. As 1 foot = 12 inches then 4 inches is $^4/_{12}$ feet = $^1/_3$ feet = **0.33 feet**.
6c	A	46cm³	The volume of the cylinder = 3 × the volume of the cone. Therefore, the volume of the cone = $^1/_3$ × the volume of the cylinder = $^1/_3$ × 138 = **46cm³**.
6d	A	0.555kg	555,000mg = 555g = **0.555kg**.
6e	E	4	A cuboid has 6 face and on this cube there is a 1 or a 2 present on all faces. If the number 1 is written on 2 of the faces then 2 must be written on the other **4** faces.

Test 7, pages 49-56

Question		Answer	Explanation
1a	B	1,050ml	The jug shows 1.05l, which is **1,050ml**.
1b	C	70%	The jug is $^{1,050}/_{1,500}$ × 100 = **70%** filled to capacity with water.
1c	E	0.9 litres	$^{3}/_{5}$ × 1.5 = **0.9 litres**.
1d	A	450ml	600ml - 150ml = **450ml**.
1e	C	3 pints	If 1 pint ≈ 500ml then 1,500ml ≈ 1500 ÷ 500 = **3 pints**.
2a	E	$^{3}/_{7}$	10, 15 and 21 are triangular numbers, which is 3 out of the 7 numbers = $^{3}/_{7}$.
2b	C	$^{2}/_{7}$	4 and 25 are squared numbers, which is 2 out of the 7 numbers = $^{2}/_{7}$.
2c	E	$^{1}/_{7}$	27 is a cubed number, which is 1 out of the 7 numbers = $^{1}/_{7}$.
2d	A	XXXI	In Roman numerals, X = 10 and I = 1. Therefore, 31 in Roman numerals is **XXXI**.
2e	B	19	The average of the counter values = sum of values ÷ number of values = (27 + 31 + 15 + 10 + 4 + 25 + 21) ÷ 7 = 133 ÷ 7 = **19**.
3a	A	6	A regular hexagon has **6** lines of symmetry.
3b	C	QR	Line **QR** is parallel to line TU.
3c	D	T	Point **T** is South of point P.
3d	A	30°	Interior angles in a hexagon sum to 720°. Each interior angle is therefore, 720° ÷ 6 = 120°. X = 120° - 90° = **30°**.
3e	B	540mm	The perimeter of the hexagon = 6 × 9 = 54cm = **540mm**.

Question		Answer	Explanation
4a	D	**13:2**	The ratio of the output to number machine 3 to the input to number machine 3 is 65:10 = **13:2**.
4b	B	**15**	Working forwards from the input, $\frac{1}{3} - \frac{1}{8} = (\frac{1}{3} \times \frac{8}{8}) - (\frac{1}{8} \times \frac{3}{3}) = \frac{8}{24} - \frac{3}{24} = \frac{5}{24}$. $\frac{5}{24} \times 72 = \mathbf{15}$, which is the output.
4c	A	**26.5**	Working backwards from the output, 11.87 + 14.63 = **26.5**, which is the input.
4d	B	**6**	Writing number machine 3 out as an equation gives, $(10 + 3^2 - ?) \times 5 = 65$. This simplifies to $(19 - ?) \times 5 = 65$. Dividing both sides by 5 gives $19 - ? = 65 \div 5$. Therefore, $19 - ? = 13$. $? = 19 - 13 = \mathbf{6}$.
4e	D	**11.9**	Since the question asks for 11.87 to be rounded to the nearest tenth, the hundredth column must be considered. As 7 is greater than or equal to 5, the digit in the tenths column must be round up. Therefore, 11.87 is **11.9** to the nearest tenth.
5a	E	**W**	Point **W** is directly West of the police station.
5b	A	**(-4,-2)**	The Hospital is at coordinates **(-4, -2)**.
5c	A	**X**	If the supermarket at coordinates (3, 3) is moved 7 units left and 2 units up it will move to coordinates (-4, 5). Point **X** at coordinates (-2, 4) is closest to (-4, 5).
5d	B	**(1,0)**	The police station at coordinates (5, 0) is reflected in the line x = 3. Its new coordinates will be **(1, 0)**.
5e	C	**7.5km**	1 mile ≈ 2km. Therefore, 3.75 miles is approximately 2 × 3.75 = **7.5km**.
6a	E	**4**	The highest common factor (HCF) of 8 and 44 is **4**.
6b	E	**280**	-28 × -10 = **280**.
6c	A	**72**	Range = largest value - smallest value = 44 - (-28) = 44 + 28 = **72**.
6d	D	**62**	Each term in the number sequence is found by adding 18 onto the previous term. The sixth term is therefore 44 + 18 = **62**.
6e	A	**15**	The equation (-10 + Y) × 2 = 10 can be written Divide both sides by 2: -10 + Y = $\frac{10}{2}$ = 5 Add 10 to both sides: Y = 5 + 10 = **15**.

Test 8, pages 57-64

Question	Answer		Explanation
1a	D	Thursday	If 9th February is a Tuesday, then the 18th February, which is nine days later will be on a **Thursday**.
1b	C	6:45 AM	The left clock face shows **6:45 AM**.
1c	E	16:10	The right clock face shows 4:10 PM, which is **16:10**.
1d	C	0.89cm	The minute hand is 28.5mm in length = 2.85cm. The minute hand is 2.85 - 1.96 = **0.89cm** longer than the hour hand.
1e	E	3.225cm	The diameter is 6.45cm and the radius = 6.45 ÷ 2 = **3.225cm**.
2a	E	10°C	The range of temperatures is the largest value - the smallest value = 20°C - 10°C = **10°C**.
2b	A	13°C	The mode is the temperature which occurs with the highest frequency = **13°C**.
2c	A	5	√400°C = 20°C, which was recorded on day **5**.
2d	C	32°C	The temperature on day 1 was 10°C, which is **32°C** above minus 22°C.
2e	C	23°C	A 15% increase on 20°C is $\frac{115}{100} \times 20$ = **23°C**.
3a	D	£5.30	There is a total of (28 × 5p) + (9 × 10p) + (3 × 100p) = 140p + 90p + 300p = 530p = **£5.30** in the money box.
3b	B	7 : 3	The ratio of five pence coins to other coins is 28:12 = **7:3**.
3c	A	$^7/_{10}$	There are 40 coins in total and 28 are 5 pence coins, which as a fraction is $^{28}/_{40}$ = $^7/_{10}$.
3d	C	21	If $^1/_4$ of the 5 pence coins are removed, $^3/_4$ remain, which is $^3/_4 \times 28$ = **21**.
3e	D	4,500cm³	Volume = length × width × height = 25 × 10 × 18 = **4,500cm³**.

Question	Answer		Explanation
4a	D	225°	Interior angles in a octagon sum to 1080°. As it's a regular octagon each interior angle equals 1080° ÷ 8 = 135°. X = 360° - 135° = **225°**
4b	C	36mm^2	The length of one side of the square = 0.9 - 0.3 = 0.6cm = 6mm. The area of the square is 6 × 6 = **36mm^2**.
4c	D	4cm	The length of one side of the regular octagon = 2.7 - 2.2 = 0.5cm. The perimeter of the octagon is 8 × 0.5 = **4cm**.
4d	B	8	A regular octagon maps onto itself 8 times when rotated 360° about its centre. Therefore, its order of rotational symmetry is **8**.
4e	A	2	**2** sides on the octagon are perpendicular to side PQ.
5a	A	24	Multiples of 6: 6, 12, 18, 24, 30, … Multiples of 8: 8, 16, 24, 32, 440, … Multiples of 12: 12, 24, 36, 48, 60, … Therefore, the lowest common multiple (LCM) of 6, 12 and 8 is **24**.
5b	B	1	From the numbers given, there is only **1** number which is a triangular number (6).
5c	C	8	$18^0 + \sqrt{49} = 1 + 7 = $ **8**.
5d	E	17	From the numbers given, **17** is the one number which can be divided by 1 and itself only. This makes it the only prime number.
5e	B	1000	17 × 60 = 1,020 = **1,000** when rounded to the nearest 100.
6a	A	(0, 5)	Point S is at coordinates **(0, 5)**.
6b	A	(3, 4)	The coordinates of point W are determined using the number machine. The input is the x coordinate of point W, which is 3. The output is the y coordinate of point W, which equals 3 × 11 = 33; 33 - 29 = 4. This gives the coordinates **(3, 4)**.
6c	B	(0, 2)	Point Q at coordinates (-2, 0) is rotated 90° clockwise about point (0, 0) to take it to coordinates **(0, 2)**.
6d	D	(-1, 1)	Point R at coordinates (-2, 4) is translated 1 unit right and 3 units down to coordinates **(-1, 1)**.
6e	D	(-1, 2)	Point U at coordinates (1, 2) is reflected in the y-axis. Its new coordinates are **(-1, 2)**.

Question	Answer		Explanation
1a	D	90,000cm^2	The square has side length 3m = 300cm. The area of the square is 300cm × 300cm = **90,000cm^2**.
1b	A	17m	The perimeter of triangle T is (2 × 7m) + 3m = 14m + 3m = **17m**.
1c	A	75°	Interior angles in a triangle sum to 180°. Therefore, X = 180° - (30° + 75°) = **75°**.
1d	D	9.5m^2	Since the question asks for 9.4868m^2 to be rounded to one decimal place, the second decimal place must be considered. As 8 is greater than or equal to 5, the digit in the first decimal place must be rounded up. Therefore, 9.4868m^2 is **9.5m^2** rounded to one decimal place.
1e	C	Square based pyramid	The shape that is formed when the net is folded up is a **square based pyramid**.
2a	D	4	**4** of the letters (E, I, E, E) have a horizontal line of symmetry.
2b	D	$^1/_3$	The probability of drawing out the letter E is $^3/_9$ = **$^1/_3$**.
2c	C	$^2/_9$	The probability of drawing out the letter R is **$^2/_9$**.
2d	B	$^1/_{36}$	The probability of drawing out a P followed by an R is $^1/_9$ × $^2/_8$ = $^2/_{72}$ = **$^1/_{36}$**.
2e	E	4:5	The ratio of vowels (E, I, E, E) to non vowels (P, R, M, T, R) is **4:5**.
3a	B	95	The score Gideon obtains is (2 × 5) + (1 × 10) + (3 × 25) = 10 + 10 + 75 = **95**.
3b	C	25	The mode score is the one that occurs with the highest frequency, which is **25**.
3c	E	66.7%	4 of the 6 hoops landed in regions worth more than 5 points, which is $^4/_6$ × 100 = **66.7%**.
3d	D	6.7cm	The radius of a circular hoop is 3.35cm, so its diameter is 2 × 3.35 = **6.7cm**.
3e	B	210	The overall score is 6 × 35 = **210**.

Question		Answer	Explanation
4a	D	1	The only prime factor of 69 is 23.
4b	A	$\frac{1}{2}$	4 of the 8 numbers are prime numbers (2, 5, 19, 23), which as a fraction is $\frac{4}{8} = \frac{1}{2}$.
4c	E	25%	2 of the 8 numbers are square numbers (4, 16), which as a percentage is $\frac{2}{8} \times 100 = \mathbf{25\%}$.
4d	E	13	To find the median we have to arrange the numbers in ascending numerical order, which is 2, 4, 5, 10, 16, 19, 23, 27. The median is half way between the fourth value, which is 10 and the fifth value, which is 16. Therefore, the median is $(10 + 16) \div 2 = \mathbf{13}$.
4e	D	80	Multiples of 5: 5, 10, 15, 20, 25, 30, 35, 40, 45, 50, 55, 60, 65, 70, 75, 80, 85, ... Multiples of 10: 10, 20, 30, 40, 50, 60, 70, 80, 90, ... Multiples of 16: 16, 32, 48, 64, 80, 96, ... Therefore, the lowest common multiple (LCM) of 5, 10 and 16 is **80**.
5a	E	108 min	1.8 hr = 1.8 × 60 = **108 min**
5b	E	11:33 AM	Biyu finishes having breakfast 38 + 40 = 78 minutes after leaving home at 10:15 AM, which is at **11:33 AM**.
5c	C	£22.67	3 × £50 = £150 £150 - £127.33 = **£22.67**
5d	B	180 oz	The shopping weighed 4.5kg = 4500g. As 1 ounce ≈ 25 grams, 4500g ≈ $\frac{4500}{25}$ = **180 oz**.
5e	E	312 seconds	5.2 minutes = 5.2 × 60 = **312 seconds**.
6a	E	75	The sum of the first five terms is 25 + 20 + 15 + 10 + 5 = **75**.
6b	B	40%	2 of the 5 numbers in the sequence (15 and 25) are odd and greater than or equal to 10, which as a percentage is $\frac{2}{5} \times 100 = \mathbf{40\%}$.
6c	A	0	Each term in the number sequence is found by subtracting 5 from the previous term. Therefore, the sixth term is 5 - 5 = **0**.
6d	C	-5	As each term in the number sequence can be found by subtracting 5 from the previous term, the seventh term is 0 - 5 = **-5**.
6e	D	2	The first term in the sequence is 25 so 25 ÷ X = 12.25. Therefore, X = 25 ÷ 12.25 = **2**.

Test 10, pages 73-80

Question		Answer	Explanation
1a	E	£78	Hayley should receive 13 ÷ (13 + 2 + 5) × £120 = 13 ÷ 20 × £120 = **£78**.
1b	D	£18	Sam should receive 5 ÷ 20 × £120 = £30 and David should receive 2 ÷ 20 × £120 = £12. Therefore, Sam should receive £30 - £12 = **£18** more than David.
1c	A	£84	70% of £120 = $\frac{70}{100}$ × £120 = **£84**.
1d	E	$\frac{1}{5}$	$\frac{24}{120}$ = $\frac{1}{5}$.
1e	C	£869.47	Y + £55.28 = £924.75; Y = £924.75 - £55.28 = **£869.47**.
2a	A	135°	Angle y = 180° - 45° = **135°**.
2b	D	1.5cm	The diameter of the circle is 3cm. The radius of the circle is 3 ÷ 2 = **1.5cm**.
2c	A	(-5, 4)	Point P is at coordinates **(-5, 4)**.
2d	B	14cm	The perimeter of the rectangle is (2 × 4) + (2 × 3) = 8 + 6 = **14cm**.
2e	D	(-2, -2)	If point R at coordinates (-1, 1) is translated 3 units down and 1 unit left then its new coordinates will be **(-2, -2)**.
3a	E	1.55kg	The first set of scales shows **1.55kg**.
3b	D	1,100g	The weight shown on the second set of scales is 0.9kg = 900g, which is **1,100g** less than 2,000g.
3c	C	6.4kg	6,389g = 6.389kg = **6.4kg** to one decimal place.
3d	E	35lbs	As 14 pounds (lbs) ≈ 6kg, 15kg ≈ (15 × 14) ÷ 6 = **35lbs**.
3e	B	5³g	(5 × 5 × 5)g in index form is **5³g**.

Test 10, pages 73-80

Question		Answer	Explanation
4a	C	15	The range is the largest value minus the smallest value = 15 - 0 = **15**.
4b	D	0	The even numbered terms in the sequence are obtained by multiplying the previous even numbered term by 2. Therefore, the eighth term is 12 × 2 = 24. The probability of the eighth term being 7 is **0**.
4c	E	20	The odd numbered terms in the number sequence are obtained by adding 5 onto the previous odd numbered term. Therefore, the ninth term = 15 + 5 = **20**.
4d	B	4	**4** of the 7 numbers are triangular numbers (3, 6, 10, 15).
4e	D	3	**3** of terms 2 to 6 in the sequence are factors of 36 and 60, these are 3, 6 and 12.
5a	B	3	**3** households own 3 cars.
5b	E	28	(0 × 13) + (1 × 9) + (2 × 5) + (3 × 3) = 0 + 9 + 10 + 9 = **28** cars were owned in total.
5c	B	$^{17}/_{30}$	17 out of the 30 households, which can be expressed as $^{17}/_{30}$, owned at least one car.
5d	C	1	The median number of cars owned per household is **1**, this is half way between the 15th and 16th terms, which are both 1.
5e	A	0	The mode number of cars owned per household is the number which occurs with the highest frequency, which is **0** cars.
6a	D	8cm	$V = l \times b \times h$; $h = V \div (l \times b)$. Therefore, $h = 1280 \div (16 \times 10) = $ **8cm**.
6b	B	320cm³	1280 - 960 = **320cm³**.
6c	B	72	A cuboid has 8 vertices, so 9 cuboids have 9 × 8 = **72** vertices.
6d	A	48	A tetrahedron has 6 edges, so 8 tetrahedrons have 8 × 6 = **48** edges.
6e	C	5,440cm³	(2 × 1280) + (3 × 960) = 2560 + 2880 = **5,440cm³**.

Other Titles in the First Past The Post® Series

Numerical Reasoning: Quick-Fire

The numerical reasoning section of most 11 plus and Common Entrance exams contains multi-part questions, which are designed to test the candidate's raw mathematical ability. This series is tailored towards the Centre for Evaluation and Monitoring (CEM) Numerical Reasoning assessments but provides invaluable practice for all exam boards. Each book contains 10 tests, each of which comprises 20 questions and is designed to be completed in six minutes. Full answers and explanations are included. Each book allows access to our Peer-Compare™ Online system, which assesses the candidate's performance anonymously on a question-by-question basis.

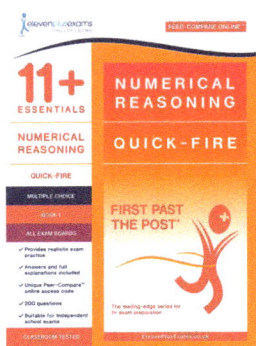

Multiple Choice

Multiple choice books provide the candidate with several options from which to choose when answering each question. This catches some candidates out by giving plausible options alongside the correct answer.

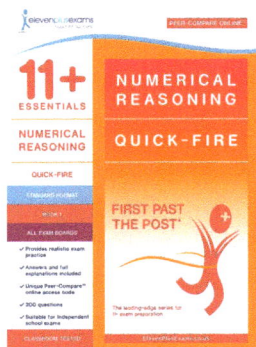

Standard Format

Standard format books do not provide the candidate with any options to choose from when answering; candidates must instead write the answer themselves in the space provided. This is challenging for candidates who rely on a process of elimination when answering multiple choice questions.

Other Titles in the First Past The Post® Series

Numerical Reasoning: Multi-Part

The numerical reasoning section of most 11 plus and Common Entrance exams contains multi-part questions, which require several conclusions to be drawn from the same initial information. This series is tailored towards the Centre for Evaluation and Monitoring (CEM) Numerical Reasoning assessments but provides invaluable practice for all exam boards. Full answers and explanations are included. Each book allows access to our Peer-Compare™ Online system, which assesses the candidate's performance anonymously on a question-by-question basis.

Multiple Choice

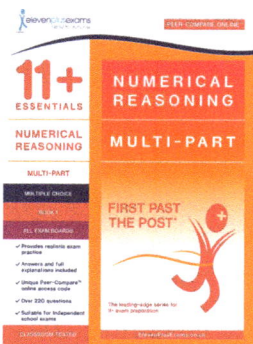

Multiple choice books provide the candidate with several options from which to choose when answering each question. This catches some candidates out by giving plausible options alongside the correct answer. Each book contains 10 tests, each of which comprises six multi-part questions, each with five parts. Each test is designed to be completed in 15 minutes.

Standard Format

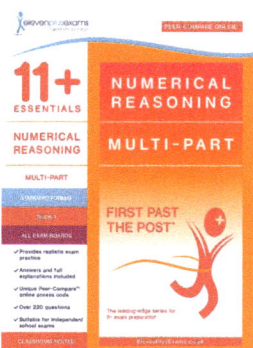

Standard format books do not provide the candidate with any options to choose from when answering; candidates must instead write the answer themselves in the space provided. This is challenging for candidates who rely on a process of elimination when answering multiple choice questions. Each book contains 10 tests, each of which comprises five multi-part questions. Each test is designed to be completed in 20 minutes.

Other Titles in the First Past The Post® Series

Mathematics: Mental Arithmetic

Mental arithmetic is a core skill tested by all 11 plus and Common Entrance exams. These books each comprise 20 tests, and each test contains 30 questions and is designed to be completed in 10 minutes. By working through this series, a candidate can develop the key skills needed to excel in numerical reasoning and mathematics and the confidence needed to tackle exam questions under time pressure. Full answers and explanations are included.

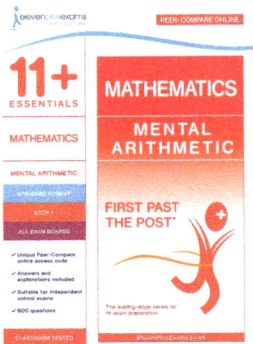

Each test can be marked and evaluated via our Peer-Compare™ Online system, which assesses the candidate's performance anonymously on a question-by-question basis. This helps identify areas for improvement and benchmarks the candidate's score against that of others who have taken the same tests.

Other Titles in the First Past The Post® Series

Mathematics: Worded Problems

The majority of 11 plus and Common Entrance exams test mathematical skills through complex, worded questions. These test the candidate's ability to extract information from the question as much as they test their actual mathematical ability, and it is this that often catches candidates out. This series is designed to build confidence in working through worded questions so that candidates can tackle them under time pressure in the real exam. Full answers and explanations are included.

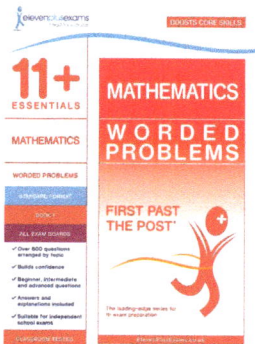

Each book in this series comprises 14 chapters, each of which focuses on a different topic. Within each chapter, there are 15 beginner questions, 15 intermediate questions and 15 advanced questions.

Other Titles in the First Past The Post® Series

Mathematics: Dictionary Plus

This book is an indispensable companion to our practice papers and workbooks, containing definitions of key mathematical concepts in accessible language. Each definition is accompanied by a worked, illustrated example and a series of questions to ensure a thorough understanding of its practical applications. The questions have two tiers of difficulty: 'Test yourself' and 'Challenge yourself'. Full answers are included.

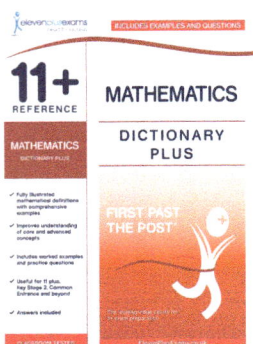

This is a comprehensive reference volume, invaluable for all students at 11 plus and Common Entrance exams, Key Stage 2 and beyond.